THE
DREAM
MACHINE

LIONCREST
PUBLISHING

THE DREAM MACHINE

*A Leader's Guide to Creating Teams of High Performers
Who Achieve Extraordinary Outcomes*

ISBN 978-1-5445-2206-7 *Hardcover*
         978-1-5445-2205-0 *Paperback*
         978-1-5445-2204-3 *Ebook*

THE
DREAM
MACHINE

A LEADER'S GUIDE TO CREATING TEAMS
OF **HIGH PERFORMERS** WHO ACHIEVE
EXTRAORDINARY OUTCOMES

DANE ESPEGARD

For my wife, Brookelynn,

and our daughters, Elin and Izzi.

CONTENTS

INTRODUCTION

"Here we go."

This is my go-to phrase when I open meetings. It's my way to frame what is about to happen next as a journey.

And so, it's an appropriate statement to open this book with too. Because when used with intention, the process laid out here is more than words on a page, bound together by a nice-looking cover with a snappy title. You're about to begin a life-changing process of creating dreams for yourself, and for the people you work with, which I call *The Dream Machine*.

Let me start with some backstory...

Dreams for most people are a fluffy concept. They seem cartoonishly wistful. Or they are one-day, someday, if-only ideas that float in hazy thought bubbles. They can be inspired ideas a person may or may not accomplish. Or, maybe they're itemized and more formally scrawled on a handwritten bucket list on a notepad and then pinned to a corkboard, marked by a fading coffee cup ring.

I once thought of them that way too. But now, I'm serious about dreams. They make life miraculous. They give meaning to each moment. They are why I get up in the morning.

In my company and social circle, I've become well-known as "the dreams guy," and so my radar is keenly tuned to everything dreams. I hear a lot of stories of dreams achieved. Many of them I share in this book. But I also hear a lot of stories of dreams unfulfilled. These stories are both heartbreaking and sobering, and the reason this book had to be written.

Take Jane, a close family friend. She and her husband worked extremely hard in their careers. They were smart with their money. They planned to travel the world in their retirement. As they were retiring, Jane's husband was diagnosed with Alzheimer's. He declined quickly. The dream life the couple had worked so hard for was gone.

Jane and her husband's story is not too far from the dashed someday dreams my grandparents experienced. I never had the opportunity to meet my maternal grandmother because she passed when she was fifty-four after a battle with cancer. My mother said that before she died she'd talked a lot about traveling the world. When her and my grandfather talked about travel plans, he would often say "yeah, someday." My grandfather was a farmer who worked long hours. I believe he was genuine in his "someday" comments, but her passing came too soon. It didn't give either of them the opportunity to live out her dreams.

So many people spend their lives working for a life that they will be able to live in the future. This book is the antithesis of the live-to-work approach. And it's why I'm so passionate about the concepts in this book. The dreams system it features brings meaning to the now. It's about a new way to live where dreams are not a "maybe someday" idea.

Many people will tell you they dream of a safe and abundant future for their children. They work hard so they can buy a nice home in a secure neighborhood, pay for their kids' college education, and then enjoy a comfortable retirement and perhaps then have the resources to travel.

But what would happen if the people who planned the so-called "dream" retirement took it sooner? Why not travel now? Where would you go? Who would you take? Spouse? Kids? Grandkids?

What else? Would you write a book? Volunteer? Sing in a band? Cut a single or make an album? How about learn to fly? Perhaps you'd like to learn to speak Mandarin.

What's the one thing you say you want to do someday but you don't truly have a plan for? Or maybe your "someday" idea keeps moving? What's the one thing you have said you always wanted to do but have never had the opportunity to start because you didn't have time, or money, or a partner to do it with?

How much better would life be if all those things you dreamed of—and that may have been relegated to retirement—could start this weekend? Who would you inspire with your songs? Your book? What would be possible if you could captain your own boat, fly your own plane, make new friends in foreign lands where they don't speak English?

I always say when there is hope in the future, there is power in the present. My dream is that with this book, you'll come to know this too if you're not there already.

I've found that when people get serious about dreams, and write them on a list, commit to them with an action plan, or share their wild inspired ideas with a friend or partner, those dreams have a greater chance of becoming a reality. When you or a person you know checks off and celebrates even just one dream, it can easily become a positive addiction.

And when someone is on a team that is centered around the concept of dreams, the individual has an encouraging environment where their dreams thrive, multiply, and happen faster.

I titled this book *The Dream Machine* for this reason. I pursued and lived my dreams out loud within my organization. It became contagious at work. Then my management team and I built on it and it turned into a full-fledged culture of pursuing your dreams.

I've become the guy who initiated one simple process that has continued to grow organically. It's like I pushed one button on a machine and it made a bunch of widgets turn and triggered a number of systems to start.

Today, my team is regularly checking dreams off their list and posting them to social media. Then the people in their circles are enlivened. Once you start living your dreams it's difficult to stop. Naturally, the people around you take notice and get inspired too.

Since launching my first dream-planning workshop in 2013, I've watched hundreds of my teammates (many of whom are my very good friends) achieve dreams that were once only inspired ideas that they had no real plans to make happen. Running marathons. Building 4,000-square-foot dream homes. Launching epic side businesses. Traveling to exotic far-off places they never thought possible.

Some have achieved the unexpected. They have inspired community groups and taken on leading them. Others raised their personal standards in their role as husband, wife, father, or mother. Many more have lives they once didn't imagine were possible.

For me, I've accomplished hundreds of dreams of my own, such as traveling to places like Costa Rica and the Amalfi Coast in Italy, running a marathon, and writing this book. (So thank you for helping me check off another dream fulfilled.)

Up until I wrote this book, I didn't fully grasp the magnitude of how a simple dream-planning system that I deployed back in 2013 has positively transformed the lives of hundreds of people.

This story, however, almost never happened.

WHY DREAMS?

After I graduated high school, and before attending the University of Wisconsin-Madison, I fell into an entry-level sales position with Vector Marketing where I learned to sell Cutco cutlery doing in-home presentations.

I had a great experience with the company, learning invaluable skills such as communication, time management, perseverance, dealing with rejection, and a multitude of other things that the sales process teaches you. I had great mentors and they taught me invaluable leadership skills.

After graduating from college, I was promoted to the position of District Manager. I built a results-producing team and we were nationally competitive in our first year. Shortly after, I was promoted to Division Manager, where I built my second team from scratch in Omaha, Nebraska. My results were better than my first effort, but then I hit a wall. My business flatlined.

It was the worst business sales plateau I've ever experienced. I considered a career change. I was twenty-six years old and had peaked early. Revenues plateaued and my frustration grew. My usual strategy of cranking up the hours, grinding harder, and driving my team more rigorously was no longer an effective way to produce results.

How's this happening? I thought. *What's going on? Maybe I need to just switch companies?* But then I remembered a quote from one of my earliest business mentors: "People think switching companies will fix their problems but what they forget is that they are the common denominator."

Maybe leaving wasn't the answer? I'd likely repeat this same pattern somewhere else. Knowing this, I stuck it out until our annual national event for managers. My plan was to connect with other leaders in my organization to see what I was doing wrong.

So, I went there with an open mind seeking support from other managers. I did my best to speak to as many of them as I could in an effort to figure out what I was doing wrong. What I took away from every successful leader I spoke to was that they had a fierce commitment to their personal growth.

For the first time I got straight with myself. Up to that point, I'd skated up the corporate ladder on energy and charisma alone. I was a hard worker, but I didn't spend enough time getting intentional and prescriptive about what skills I needed to improve, and actually spend the time to develop the skill. My natural ability couldn't take me where I wanted to go. In my mind, there was a massive gap between where I was and where I wanted to be. I've since found, I'm not the only leader this has happened to. Can you relate?

I needed to work on myself and on my business, I thought, not just expect to grow every year without putting in work on me. So immediately I committed to a new routine. It included a new morning ritual of exercise, reading, intentional thought, and checking in with my goals. My goal became to read thirty books and put the most valuable tools I learned into action immediately. I read a lot of books on topics of personal development, standards, and team cultures. I started there.

Not long after, I had the opportunity to make a lateral move, to start from scratch to build a new team in a new larger territory. Since I'd already built two organizations at that point, I recognized that an organization's culture, whether or not you're intentional about it, is created by its leaders.

So I thought deeply about how to engineer a unique culture, one that I would be excited to be a part of. I envisioned a culture that embraced the truism:

We don't have a work life and a personal life. We have ONE life.

In 2012, I made a commitment that I would build a team where people could be themselves, where they knew the names of my wife and kids. To start, I gave my new team an aspirational name.

We would be the "North Star Dream Team." To get there I asked myself, "How do I accomplish that?" That's when I landed on dreams as the concept that was the way forward.

THE ASTONISHING RESULTS
THAT DREAMING AT WORK PRODUCES

When I thought about the North Star Dream Team I wanted to create, I realized turnover was always going to be a part of team building. But I stopped playing defense and decided to play offense.

In direct sales, it's easy to feel like high turnover is just in our industry, but from interacting with other business owners I found that every business struggles with turnover. So I changed my outlook.

Every employee at every business is there temporarily; even if it's a decade, most people will move on. So, if someone is going to be with me temporarily, I'd like them to be fully engaged and alive while they are with me. I'd rather have a teammate who is fully engaged in their work for two years than someone who does a mediocre job for four years.

As I write this book, the world is coming out of the COVID-19 pandemic where most businesses have shifted to work from home. Most companies are keeping a portion of their workforce working virtually. This is leading to a more competitive job market for the top talent. People have the ability to work from home for any organization across the globe. The normal extras like free dry cleaning or free lunch Friday don't have the same impact.

Back then, I did not have these concerns. I was simply trying to figure out: how can I connect my team's actions today to their long-term goals?

Most people are constantly deciding on their future. And I knew that if I could help each teammate get clear on their purpose inside the company, it would alleviate this constant battle with long-term uncertainty. It would give them more energy to pursue a better today and tomorrow.

But, I wondered, what type of structure would my team need to have in place to make this happen?

When I pondered the answer to this question, I remembered back to a corporate event for District and Division Managers that I had attended in 2007. It was there I met Australian motivational speaker Matthew Kelly (you'll hear more about him later in the book).

Kelly's talk was the beginning of my Dream Machine approach, which is based on a concept he wrote about in his book *The Dream Manager*. I built a system around the concepts and adapted them over the last nine years. This system is what I've used to motivate and retain the thousands of salespeople I have recruited and managed.

At that corporate event in 2007, Kelly asked a room of 400 managers to write a dreams list. I typed up mine, titled it "Dane's Dream List," and filed it in a folder on my computer, but then didn't look at it for five years.

In 2012, when I was getting ready to make my lateral move to Minneapolis, I used much of my morning "think time" to get clear on how I would build differently. I went back to the original Dreams List and reviewed it. I used it as the basis to build a new one. I knew that if I wanted a culture of dream achieving in my business, it had to start with me, so I got serious this time. I built an action plan and started checking off dreams.

And then I lived my new dreams lifestyle out loud, at work, with my new team. I encouraged everyone to do the same.

The results we produced blew my mind.

The year prior to implementing the Dreams System in my Division, we produced roughly $2 million in sales in 2012. My first year implanting the system in 2013 we grew to roughly $3.5 million. Nine years later—and through three iterations of the Dream Machine method—sales grew to $7.3 million in 2020. That was the year the COVID-19 pandemic struck the US. For 2021, as I write this, we're forecasting $8 million in sales. The biggest factor…The Dream Machine.

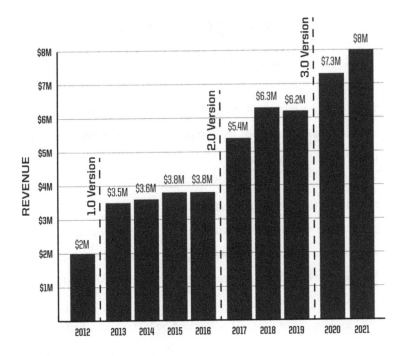

The Dream Machine system I share in this book helps people live more fulfilling lives, and in doing so brings a new dimension to work, massively expanding sales results and ensuring talent retention for the organization they work for.

While it is a people-focused concept that is designed to develop them and what they want in their lives, it also has a massive impact on a company. When implemented properly, it boosts both sales results and employee retention. And with those two ingredients anything is possible.

THE WORKPLACE (AND WORLD) NEEDS BIG DREAMERS

Dream planning isn't simply a fun hobby. Workplaces, and the world at large, need people who think big and chase their wild, inspired ideas.

I'm writing this book in the midst of the COVID-19 pandemic. This global health crisis has agitated the need for people to get clear on their purpose, to dream again, and to get serious about creating the life they had previously daydreamed about.

If you look at mental health statistics over the course of the last decades, that trend is not a positive one. While I don't believe there's ever an instant fix, working alongside thousands of people from different backgrounds and cultures, I have always seen positive movement when a person is working with purpose. They re-engage with life. Their target could be as big as purchasing their first home, or reconnecting with an estranged sibling, or as minor as journaling for thirty days straight. Either way, they've succeeded at one thing, which motivates them toward another.

The way I see it, if a workplace helps its people improve their mental disposition, that's some of the greatest work a business can do. Most people spend one-third of their life at work. If the environment at work enlivens them, wow, isn't that the best thing for a business?

When a person has a clear vision for dreams they want to achieve, they are more engaged and more resilient during challenging times. The pandemic of 2020 was difficult for many people because of the great deal of uncertainty they had to deal with. Dreams give people hope in dark times. They allow people to feel in control of much of their life.

The dream system you're about to learn is a simple way to make that happen.

People don't have a personal life and a work life. They have one life.

Companies win in business when they encourage people to live fuller lives. A dream-focused person works with more vigor, focus, and clarity. So while a dream-planning system might seem simply like a great perk for a company, it really is much more. It's necessary today. Businesses everywhere are dealing with disruption of markets caused by so many variables: technology, startups, social movements, and more.

Businesses need to innovate fast. They need teams run by people who think big and understand where they fit into the company mission. Dreams do this. They wake people up to ever-increasing levels of what's possible.

Millennials and Gen Zs, which are increasing in the workforce, are more hungry for purpose than earlier generations. They care about the contribution they're making to their company and to the world at large, and they want to be fulfilled.

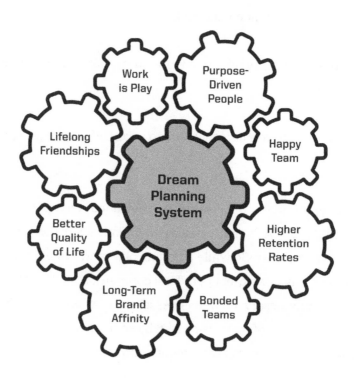

As a business owner, it has also made my job much more enjoyable, because we're not focused entirely on the sales, bottom line, and profit. My primary focus is the happiness of the people who work with me. I've found when I focus on this, every other aspect is taken care of. We have a strong focus on the numbers that make our business run, but the overall mission is to help our team members life the life of their dreams.

It's not hard to build a dream culture. When I first initiated my dream system, one of my first goals was to make it easy. I wanted a culture that was exciting for people to be around, one that kept people coming back for more. I knew that when people experience "life moments," travel to great places, or just share their motivations in life, it connects them to the people around them. Over the years, I've revised the process so any leader can replicate it.

BUILDING A DREAM MACHINE

If you currently run a business or lead a team, or plan to one day, in this book you'll learn the A to Z framework for how to bring a dream planning system to your company. My goal is to make it easy for any business to adopt. Also, I'll help you avoid the common hurdles I've encountered.

For instance, when people start dreaming, they have a tendency to hold themselves back by being too rational. So here, you'll learn phrases to use during a workshop. You'll also learn how to use what I call "thought joggers" and why they are critical, and why leading by example and sharing your stories is a key tenet of the process.

I've also found the most effective way to have people do the actual dream work is with an annual dreams workshop. So you'll learn how to lead an annual Dreams Retreat. It's a three-phase process that starts with dreamstorming, then moves to dream sharing (which includes dream stealing!) and action planning. That last component—taking action—is critical, by the way. It's why most people rarely make dreams a reality.

Last, the most thrilling aspect of dreams are the unexpected benefits that come from them. Dreams produce a reverberating effect of awesomeness that impacts leaders, teams, and the company as a whole.

But before we begin, there is one prerequisite: you must be willing to dream yourself. No leader can help anyone if they don't get serious about what's truly possible for them. And my guess is, like me, once you engage in this process, you'll discover what I did: any barrier you have between what you believe and what you can accomplish doesn't really exist. Everything is possible.

So are you ready?

Here we go.

CHAPTER 1

EMBRACE GROWTH MINDSET

WE ALL EXPERIENCE TIMES in life when someone gives us advice that seems obvious, yet it's such a departure from what we've been doing that it pivots our lives right then and there. It sends us on a new path. That's what happened to me the day I heard Matthew Kelly speak.[1]

"How are you all?" asked Kelly, our keynote speaker.

His distinct Aussie accent, such a difference from any American voice in the room, immediately grabbed my full attention. He spoke casually, stood with his hands in his pockets, but was dressed in a well-traveled business suit. His body language said, "I'm approachable, down-to-earth, and confident."

Kelly was the kind of leader I've always resonated with. He was down to earth, and the kind of guy who didn't take himself too seriously. He was super relatable, spoke about his family, and used a lot of humor to connect with the crowd. I liked him right away. Then he opened his mouth and I liked him even more.

Kelly is the author of the book *The Dream Manager*, a business narrative about how companies can achieve remarkable results by helping their employees achieve their dreams. He was hired as the keynote speaker at my company's national conference in 2007. At this annual event, District and Division Managers from seven regions gather at a cool destination to learn. That year, we were in Orlando at Disney's Contemporary Resort.

Now, these weekend events tend to be your typical corporate rollouts, with general sessions and breakouts with more hands-on training. In between there is the usual reconnecting with peers in the hallways during the allotted breaks. For two days, most of the messages were from people who were the best in our business.

Every few years the company will bring in an outsider, the highlight of the event. Kelly was that year's keynote. Little did I know, his talk would change my life.

"Once a year, I get my staff together for what I call a 'dream session,'" Kelly said. "I ask everyone to come to it with a list of one hundred personal dreams."

Kelly sauntered back and forth on the stage mocking his teammates with an affected high-pitched voice. "The new employees always moan. They say, 'How am I going to come up with one hundred dreams?'"

It was funny. The bobbing faces seated around each circular banquet grinned and nodded. And I did too.

Until that moment my life centered around one category: work.

For many years, what kept me motivated was getting the next promotion, reaching the next sales milestone, and winning contests. I couldn't imagine coming up with one hundred personal dreams or why I would want to. Goals at work? Sure. Dreams outside of work? Mostly unfathomable.

Most people are caught up in the whole work-to-live, live-to-work pattern. I was too—until that day. My mindset was: let me give my business one hundred hours a week if I need to, to get to where I want to be. I'm sure you'd agree, that's not sustainable.

Kelly's ideas on dreams made me pause and take a look at my life. I found myself asking:

- Why am I working?

- What lights me up outside of work?

- How can I enjoy what I do more?

So when I got home, Kelly's book was the first item out of my take-home corporate gift bag. I read it cover to cover.

What Kelly had gotten me to do was sit down and create my very first dreams list. I thought up one hundred dreams that I figured would be cool to accomplish someday.

After that day I went through a period where I was more energized. I went back to my team and shared the concept. Everyone was excited and connected on a different level. Sadly, that's where it stalled. I went back to my old way of doing things and the dreams concept continued to just live on my computer.

Yet, my business outperformed all years prior to that year. Creating the list had given me a new perspective on why I was working. Though I put the list away, and didn't get serious about dreams until 2012, the list exercise had given me a shot of energy and new context.

I got better with my money too, because I had new focuses for it. At that point, many of them were superficial. But I also started thinking more deeply about what I'd like to invest in. I wanted to own rental properties and create passive income. I wanted to hit savings milestones. I wanted to be able to retire at a certain age.

Healthwise, before I made this first list, I had zero goals. Suddenly, the tiny belly I was already growing in my mid-twenties started to bug me. I began to wonder: "If I were my best self in the most amazing shape, what would I do—a Tough Mudder, a half-marathon?"

Before making my dreams list, I had been winning at work, but sacrificing success in other areas. Okay, honestly, I wasn't accomplishing much personally. It was all about career and financial success. For the first time, I noticed that I always had ideas of what I wanted, but I never got clear on them.

For instance, I always told myself, "Yeah, I'll get married. I'm going to have kids." But I didn't dig much deeper. I had never considered: What kind of marriage do I want to be in? What kind of father do I want to be? And, what processes do I need in place to follow through?

I found that once I started this type of deeper thinking, once I put a few dreams on a list, regardless of the fact that I didn't look at this first list every day, I was a little more driven.

I've discovered this is true for most people. When you put pen to paper, the odds increase and you're more likely to achieve what you intend. I began checking dreams off in all areas of my life. Consequently, I unlocked a deeper level of fulfillment. I experienced a renewed vigor with life. And naturally, this caused me to dream and achieve more.

Eventually, I became addicted to dreams as a way of life. I became a regular dreamer and achiever of those dreams. I wanted everyone to experience the same.

But I also knew that talk of dreams at work could be met with resistance. In a sensible, traditionally driven business environment there was no place for something so woo-woo. That old-school pinstripe suit thinking doesn't allow unicorns and magic rainbows into the mahogany formality of the boardroom.

So, to be successful in launching a dream system or talking about dreams, a culture itself needs to be ready for it. One prerequisite to establishing a dream-planning system at any workplace is that the culture must embrace a growth mindset and growth language first.

A GROWTH-MINDED CULTURE IS A DREAMS PREREQUISITE

I n 2018 cross-cultural psychologist Michelle Gelfand gave a TEDx talk in Palo Alto called "The Secret Life of Social Norms," where she discussed her research and insights into the cultural differences between tight and loose cultures.[2] Gelfand explained that any culture can be classified as either tight or loose or falling somewhere between that range.

A tight culture is classified as any group that is rigid and rule-based, and has strict punishments for behaviors. Singapore is a great example of a tight culture. There you would never see a person jaywalk like New Yorkers do. Walking naked in your house is illegal too, which means I'm definitely not moving there anytime soon. They've also banned gum from the entire country.

At the other end of the spectrum is a country like New Zealand. They have a more lax approach to life with a flip-flop sporting, beach bumming, wind-surfing on the weekend attitude. A New Zealand dude, who is purportedly a retired university lecturer, roams the streets in a wizard hat and was dubbed the Wizard of New Zealand. His mandate is to lift spirits and engage with strangers to get them to have fun. New Zealand has a loose culture.

Any culture falls somewhere on the tight-to-loose spectrum, which dictates the overall group behavior and the formation of social norms. Workplaces can be classified this way too. At any company with a rigid attitude like Singapore, a growth mindset is likely to be absent.

Many businesses are tight cultures with strict hierarchies where personal lives are separate. I'm sure you'd agree that many post-industrial revolution management models popular in the last century are still alive today in many organizations. Yet we also know that businesses need speed and innovation today, making "growth mindset" one of the biggest buzzwords in the business media and consulting circles. "Your people must be growth-minded," we hear from executive management teams and thought leaders across disciplines.

I'm sure you'd agree, a growth mindset is an imperative in a business landscape that's fraught with disruption caused by technological innovations, social movements, and now worldwide pandemics. When you're experiencing asymmetrical warfare in business, the defense is to train your people to adapt fast.

Big thinkers are more resilient, they move fast, and they adjust to their environments as needed. They also enjoy their work far more because they have targets to aim for. Progress unlocks power, and certainly fulfillment too.

"You're either growing or you're dying." Tony Robbins, one of the world's top performance coaches, motivational speakers, and philanthropists, is well-known for saying this phrase. There's really no better way to explain the connection between growth and fulfillment.

The first time I heard him say this, I was in a crowd of about 4,000 while attending one of his *Unleash the Power Within* seminars. This was early on in my career; I was in my mid-twenties at the time. Personal development seminars like this are part of my company's culture. And I am glad they are, because being part of this culture turned me into a growth-minded, optimistic thinker very early on.

That, plus growing up in a family of dream achievers. My parents opened a massively successful daycare business when I was a kid. So, I was exposed to an optimistic "anything is possible" attitude early in life.

Then I joined Cutco at eighteen. It was a great first job out of high school for me due to its strong culture of personal growth. So I was exposed to many training and development and advancement opportunities at a very young age. I valued each occasion to learn and grow, and Cutco's culture fortified an early love of personal development.

At that first Robbins seminar, I remember thinking that Tony made a lot of practical sense.

"People ask me: what does it take to be happy?" he said. The man is a titan on stage, and has an equally giant heart.

"I'll give that to you in one word," he said, then paused for a beat with his finger angled in the air toward the crowd. "Progress!" he finished. "Progress equals happiness."

Tony's right.

I reflected on times where I'd felt most alive in the past. When I learned how to ride a bike at four. Or when I mastered a new routine in Odyssey of the Mind, which was a problem-solving game I used to participate in as a kid. The progress I made at Cutco working toward the next sales milestone also always brought me joy.

People feel most fulfilled when they are growing. It's a basic operating principle in human psychology. Abraham Maslow, an American psychologist who created Maslow's Hierarchy of Needs, is well-known for establishing this principle.[3]

Maslow's theory of psychological health shows how a person's behavior is always motivated by a certain set of needs. His research showed that every person is always on a growth trajectory. When a person's needs for food, shelter, and belonging are met, they are most motivated by feeling fulfilled by what they do.

The highest stage to reach is self-actualization, where giving back to the world by contributing gifts becomes fundamental. So every person is always evolving. When our circumstances block our growth, or life remains the same for too long, we stagnate and feel unhappy.

Carl Rogers was another American psychologist who founded the humanistic approach to psychology in the mid-twentieth century. His popular theory was based on growth potential. His research showed that people's aim is constantly to integrate their "real self"—who they are now—with their "ideal self"—who they wish to be.

Many modern-day psychologists and thought leaders like Tony Robbins draw from these early psychologists. The growth-fulfillment connection has been proven many times over. It's a scientific tenet as true as gravity.

I made the growth-fulfillment connection early on, so when I heard Matthew Kelly's talk in my early years, and he said, "When there's hope in the future, there's power in the present," it made complete sense.

Until I heard Kelly, however, the idea had remained conceptual. I had always looked at goal-setting as a task that needed to be done but never understood its true value. I neither embodied the whole fulfillment equals growth equation, nor had an implementation plan to ensure I was always growing.

Up to this point, I had been amassing tools, but leaving them on the workbench mostly unused. A man with a Skilsaw and brand-name power tools is not much of a carpenter if he never goes into his workshop. I see this with many people today. It used to be my approach too. In our digitized interconnected high-tech world there's more information coming at us than ever before. It's easy to get overloaded by inputs and stop there because there is so much pulling on our attention.

Once you embody a practice that makes your life better, you can't go back to the way you were before. That's what happened to me after I authored my first dream list. It was my launching point to a new way of living.

But still, I wasn't intentional enough about my dreams yet. It wasn't until 2012 that I committed to dreams as a lifestyle focus and brought it to work.

BOAT LIVING IN THAILAND, EUROPEAN BREAKFASTS, AND SCREECHING MONKEYS

It was 2012 when Brookelynn and I held our first intentional dream-planning session on New Year's Eve heading into 2013. We made a big commitment, saying to each other, "Okay, this is the way that we're going to live our lives." That year, we both accomplished many dreams that were once seemingly impossible ideas.

One of the most memorable early dreams that Brookelynn helped me check off my list was living on a sailboat in Thailand. We'd planned a dream trip to Thailand and she knew "live on a sailboat for a week" was on my list.

One night before the trip, we were casually chatting about our work days in the kitchen and she said, "By the way, I booked us a three-night stay on a sailboat with a captain and cook for when we're in Thailand."

"Are you serious?" I said.

Brookelynn gets seasick. She'd never been on a cruise. Never wanted to be on one either.

For three days we lived on a sailboat anchored just off the island of Koh Lipe in the Andaman Sea off the southwest coast of Thailand.

From the moment we left Phuket on a six-hour speed boat ride to get to the island, we entered a life of luxury. Our captain was a friendly man from Slovenia. The sailboat adventure business was this man's retirement dream; his dream helped us fulfill ours—a synchronicity that I would come to learn happens often in dream work.

Every morning, we'd have coffee on deck with a homemade European breakfast, while staring beyond the bow of the boat and an expanse of tropical water. There were only two other sailboats sharing the glistening expanse of azure blue. During that trip, we also went hiking on a nearby uninhabited island. As the sun was setting, we summited the island's peak to soak in some beautiful views. As we made our way back down, we got lost and momentarily stuck. The sounds of screeching monkeys were all that we could hear. We found our way down as the sun disappeared, a terrifying experience that to this day is one of the best stories from that trip.

The experience was everything I thought it would be, except cheaper. When I originally wrote it on my list, it was an idea of grandeur. I thought maybe someday in the future it would happen but that it would cost a fortune. We made this dream happen for roughly $1,000 USD.

This dream seemed unrealistic because of my assumptions of cost. I've since found that when a dream goes on a list the Universe has a weird way of helping you accomplish it. This dream cost only $300 USD a night plus $60 USD for the six-hour boat ride, which nearly killed my wife.

Skydiving was another one of the first dreams I checked off my list. So was running a marathon. That same year Brookelynn completed her 500-hour yoga teacher training and purchased a yoga studio.

When Brookelynn and I made our dreams lists in 2012, I also started sharing details about our journey at work.

At that time, I had the opportunity to make a lateral move, to start from scratch building a new team in a new territory. In this new position, I knew most importantly I had to be intentional about building a growth culture.

So before I started building my team, I got clear on what my ideal culture within my organization would look like. My ideal culture was one of empowerment.

I envisioned an organization that shows people there's a different way to live. Growth was a key element and would be the starting point. Dreams were the structure that would enable follow-through on growth as a value.

To be successful in launching a dream system or talking about dreams, a culture itself needs to be ready for it. Again, one prerequisite to establishing a dream-planning system at any workplace is to embrace a growth mindset and growth language and bring this into the company culture. This ensures the dreams concept doesn't fall flat. Business itself is a numbers-driven, logical game of strategy, so building attributes into a culture to strengthen growth mindset is necessary before ever uttering the word "dream" at the office.

The rest of this chapter is an opportunity for you to do an audit on your own level of growth mindset and that of the team you want to bring the dreams concept to. You might want to consider: am I growing at a level where I am unlocking my highest level of fulfillment? If you feel energized, powerful, and enlivened at work, that's a sign that you are.

A growth mindset is needed when implementing a dream-planning system. That same growth mindset expands as a result of a dreams system. It's a perpetual cycle.

So, the idea is to build an environment, a growth-minded culture, where the dreams idea will land. Then, use a dream-planning system as the mechanism for an always growing culture of big thinkers and high achievers.

So first, is your team growth-minded enough for dreams?

THE FOUR OPERATIONAL VALUES GROWTH-MINDED TEAMS UPHOLD

A ny tight culture or loose culture has a set of tenets that underpins the way people operate. In the same way, a growth mindset has a set of values the people in it uphold that inform the way the group operates.

Four operational values hold the key to building a growth-minded team. They form the attitudes that the group upholds and works by. They are:

1. Abundance thinking versus scarcity mindset

2. Progress not perfection

3. People have one life

4. Authentic leadership

Again, as you read on, do an audit of your team and yourself.

#1: Abundance Thinking Versus Scarcity Mindset

"Get it all in before you have kids. Yep. Get it all in."

Before Brookelynn and I had kids we traveled a lot, and I can't tell you how many times I heard this statement from people. It did make us wonder. Does the fun really end when you have kids? I guess we'll find out, we thought. But we also had rebellious friends who didn't buy into the no-traveling-with-kids idea.

Justin is a close buddy and a mentor of mine who is four years older than me. He and his wife, Jennifer, demonstrated what's possible on the kid-traveling front. Like Brookelynn and me, they had a serious case of the travel bug. Then they had a baby girl and it didn't stop them.

With the baby in a sling, and passports layered in the folds of its fabric too, plus two giant suitcases packed with baby's supplies, they visited places like the Caribbean, Colombia, and Italy. I'd be flipping through my Facebook or Instagram feeds and see pictures of them posing at various world landmarks or with seriously stunning scenery in the background. There they are in Vatican City, and Greece, and at the canals of Venice, all with baby in tow.

So before we had kids, Brookelynn and I decided we'd adopt their all-in family travel lifestyle. And we have. Exotic border crossing stamps fill the pages of our kids' passports. My five-year-old daughter has been to seven countries. Her three-year-old sister is not far behind. Next on our list is Australia and New Zealand. We have already started talking with them about kangaroos and hobbits.

I'll be honest, there were a few moments where we almost bought into the "When I have kids, I can't travel" notion. Traveling with little ones often requires abnormal parenting strategies. If I go into the closet where we keep our luggage there are still traces of fishy cracker crumbs and portable packs of baby wipes. But I've found that when you're driven to accomplish a goal, you just figure it out.

It would have been easier to give in to the logic of an annual pilgrimage to Disney World or Legoland instead, or an annual summer stay at a drivable lakeside cottage rental. Those are great options too. But we didn't want to also stop what was ful-filling for us. If we didn't have friends as an example, it is highly likely that we would have abandoned our globetrotting travel aspirations during our kids' younger years.

But how sad would that have been for us and what would they be missing out on?

I feel that it is far more valuable to choose to get curious, ask why and how. Think outside, inside, around, and far away from the box. We embrace these values in every part of our family. And those skills and brain-bending attitudes transfer nicely to work too. I would argue they are also critical in business today.

Had Brookelynn and I not embraced a growth mindset we wouldn't be able to say we've seen the Eiffel Tower in Paris, ridden elephants in Chiang Mai, or partied at Carnaval in Panama. Travel has enriched my girls' worldview too. Our five-year-old is currently taking Spanish lessons. While I enjoy hearing her say "Gracias" at the dinner table, it was spectacular when she said it to a waitress at a bistro in Spain. My girls watch *Moana* but watching them play in the waves in the ocean and run through the sand is magic.

At three or five they will not, or will barely, remember the trips we have taken, but neuroscientists tell us those early years are critical for the developing brain. What impact will the taste of a *croissant au chocolat* in Paris or playing with other kids from other countries have on them as they grow? It's not hard to believe that it can only be beneficial.

Thinking beyond what the majority of people are doing, asking "is this possible?" and considering what actions to take is very powerful. Once you knock down a few dominoes, I've found, you start to think differently. You start believing, "Hey, I could probably do that," and asking, "How can I do that?"

Because our friends showed us a way forward, they inspired us to do it ourselves. And we've been able to help others, like our friends Bobby and Lera who brought their baby to Paris. That's how this system and life work.

Powerful real-life examples of people thinking differently stay with the witnesses to them. When people share at work it spreads and spurs more growth. If John in accounting loses one hundred pounds and completes a Tough Mudder, that impacts the people around him. Suddenly seemingly impossible health goals become possible for others.

Real-life examples that walk past your desk every day make bold actions more reasonable. Jennifer in HR took her kids to the Australian outback? Cool! I guess I can take my kids to see the pyramids at Chichen Itza in Mexico.

A growth-minded work culture demands that people embrace an abundance mindset. Instead of saying "We can't," they ask questions like:

- What would be awesome?

- How could we make that happen?

- Why the heck not?

If people are thinking of new possibilities in their personal life like losing thirty pounds or traveling to places they've never been, it just makes sense that they would approach business projects similarly with an "anything is possible" outlook.

This is the type of thinking to encourage at work. Especially today with more millennials and Gen Zs in the workplace. Growth is highly valued among these workers. They want people to care about them. And they want their company to care about how it impacts the world. Are we eco-friendly or environmentally friendly? What's our company doing to make a difference on the planet? How can we do more?

These groups are already abundance thinkers. So abundance thinking is also quite attractive because a new hire will think, "I can continue to grow here."

Abundance thinking is the backbone to any growth culture. When people aren't used to "anything is possible" thinking, there is work to be done. Think back to Matthew Kelly's joke about his employees: "You hear the new employees moan; they say 'how am I going to come up with one hundred dreams?'"

I tested my mom on her level of abundance thinking. I had her write a dream list and do some of the exercises you'll learn in this book. She's in her sixties and is a positive thinker by nature, but her abundance mindset needed a bit of coaxing out of her.

"Mom, around traveling, what's on your dreams list?" I asked her as we sat at a coffee shop.

"Oh, Germany!" she said. Her eyes lit up. Then she backpedaled. "Oh, that would be an expensive trip though," she said.

It wasn't the first time I heard my mom say she wanted to travel to Germany. It's where her family is from, part of her origin story. Mine too. But she was resistant to write it on a list.

"Mom, stop all that. Just keep writing." I was adamant and determined to help her shift her traditional way of approaching what's possible. Eventually, and still hesitant, she wrote the letters G-E-R-M-A-N-Y on her dream travel list. But she made a crumpled facial expression after she did it. She wasn't convinced it would happen.

Then one year later, no joke, my company had a rewards trip that I qualified for that was to Germany! So I brought her and my family along. She helped us take care of the girls and spent quality time with her grandkids in Germany. I'm not sure I would have asked her had we not wrestled about putting Germany on her travel list a year earlier.

Now she's crossed a dream off of her list that she didn't think would ever happen. It opened her mind to think more abundantly in her sixties than she even did in her younger days.

And honestly, my mom in her seventh decade is far more open than some of the twenty-year-olds I onboard at work. Abundance mindset takes determined effort. For many teams, it requires strategic layering of conversations.

The simplest way to implement abundance thinking is to make curiosity a core tenet. Again, asking questions about what would be awesome is key here.

Some people will naturally want to go to the "how" here. Resist it as it is limiting. If my mom dwelled on the "how" with her idea to visit Germany, it may never have been written on her list.

If you can maintain that as a constant conversation, you'll start to see a growth-minded environment develop.

#2: Progress Not Perfection

As the leader of my business division, I've asked myself this: "What do I want my people to remember from working with me?" Here it is:

Everybody's a work in progress, no matter what. Even if you're sixty-something years old and only a few years from retirement, or if you're a successful CEO of a business, you're still a work in progress.

I live by this mantra. As an employer, I orient my leadership around it too. My responsibility is to make sure people are growing by ensuring they feel challenged. And, that they have fun. This mindset also frames mistakes in a positive way, as forward-moving growth opportunities.

My daughters are still preschool age. But one day, when they are old enough, I will give them this advice on work: Stay at a job, or in a career, or at a company, until you feel like you're no longer growing. If that stops, go somewhere else.

I've been with my company for nineteen years. That's uncommon, especially these days. I joined because I needed a job and I've stayed because of the culture and lifestyle it offered.

Growth is synonymous with fulfillment. Everything in the universe is growing or dying. People are no different. Progress feels great. Stagnation, or worse, regression, does not. This is why so many "healthy" people struggled during COVID-19.

So the litmus test for everyone in growth-minded culture is to ask this question: is this year better than last year? The answer should be yes!

The dreams method this book lays out, when used, also ensures that everyone's personal evolution toward a better life is constant. The growth then naturally extends to the results of the company. And there is no ceiling. If implemented correctly, the growth mindset you create will create limitless results for yourself and everyone who agrees to participate. It shows up in company results.

My colleague Colleen has been with our division for four years. While I was writing this book, one day at a meeting, she told me that if it wasn't for our dreams culture she's not sure she would have stayed with our company this long.

Four years ago she wrote "backpack across Europe for three months" on her travel list. That year, she took a sabbatical and visited twelve countries. She took a helicopter ride in the Swiss Alps, rode camels in the Moroccan desert, and experienced

Oktoberfest in Germany. She came back invigorated. Immediately after the trip she broke multiple sales records. Her success has only continued.

Leaders might fear that if they talk about a greater world outside of work, they'll lose people. But in companies where growth isn't central there's often no tie-in to the bigger picture in life. Life should give work meaning, not the other way around.

Most talented twenty-somethings today are looking for their opportunity to jumpstart their career and grow to get to the next level. That's the model now.

They look for a business owner or leader who says, "Hey, if you come and work here, and you're here for two or three years, you will be a much-improved version of you when you decide to move on."

And I have to be open. I'm not going to get that type of person to work here if I'm not open to them leaving. So they might think when they start with me, they're going to be here for two years. That's fine. But I also am not afraid of them leaving because I know that I offer an attractive place to work and the likelihood is they'll stay longer.

#3: People Have One Life

Many successful organizations have some version of a growth mindset already. In other words, every organization expects to grow their bottom line. It's in the capitalist DNA. In every company, there's an expectation of growth. Quarterly results and the board meetings and the shareholders (or company owners) that ingest them are built around growing profits, sales, or market share. For any business that talks about financial growth in their next quarterly meeting, it's simple to also snap on a brief talk about the "growth of our people."

But a lot of the talk about growth of employees at work is confined to their role. In the human resources department, the metric for growth and success might be employee retention. Nobody is tracking employee days spent road tripping through our country's national parks or visiting all-inclusive resorts.

The most successful companies realize people must grow too, yes at work, but outside work as well. They look at employee growth as holistic. A person's professional growth very rarely exceeds their level of personal growth.

The old adage "leave your personal life at home" might have made sense in the manufacturing days when widget output was the priority and metric for success. You've probably heard the notion that robots don't get tired. They don't have a fight with their spouse the night before. They don't call in sick. Before there were robotic production lines, human beings were the means for production, so it made sense to instruct workers to leave their problems at home. It no longer does.

The knowledge economy is not about nuts and bolts production by hammer-wielding humans. Instead, it is about innovation and invention. If you are leveraging human creativity and problem solving, a results-seeking manager wants healthy, happy, and fulfilled humans on their team.

For instance, any team member who trains to run a marathon will have more energy at work. The same is true if they clean up their diet. Checking a major travel destination off their list will have them refreshed and ready to come back to work with new ideas, a clear mind, and a reinvigorated attitude toward challenges that they face during their work week.

I've found that when the growth of people is made to be the focus, business outcomes are achieved naturally. My division's mission statement is: "It is our job to live the life of our dreams, so we can inspire others to do the same." This mantra helps us be growth-minded.

Our cultural identity helped me build the business units I lead with less friction and resistance. I wasn't dragging anyone to tasks they needed to complete or forcing anyone to do something they were required to do. I just focused on building the growth mindset in my team, and that meant focusing on them and their wants and needs for a better life.

The results that followed were like nothing I had previously experienced, but it is a simple formula that consistently rejects the old model of management. To old-school business people it may seem like alchemy, and maybe it is. But with this strategy you can seemingly spin gold out of thin air.

#4: Authentic Leadership

Of course step one starts with you. In whatever capacity you hold as a leader in your organization, the work to implement a dream machine starts by doing the work yourself. That means you'll need to do a bit of introspection. You must also start to examine how you interact with others in the organization. Are you growth-minded and are you expanding the minds of team-mates who don't see what's possible?

I've always been attracted to the leaders in my organization who are down-to-earth, generous sharers that speak authentically about their roles at work and outside the office too. My leadership style has been shaped by many before me who spoke about being great in all areas of their lives, about evolving continuously.

I was inspired by leaders who were transparent, who were settled enough to speak candidly, a "Hey, this is me and you get to see it all" type of leader. I wanted to be that same type of leader; everybody who works for me knows who my kids are, and they know what my values are.

Great leaders believe "My job is to better the lives of my employees and customers." This attitude at the top funnels down to the team. Everyone is there to encourage, support, and make each other's lives better.

A growth-minded culture is very much driven by the leader of any team, and there has been much research to show the correlation.

Kurt Lewin, a German-American psychologist, conducted a now-famous study in 1939 that identified three distinct leadership styles: authoritarian, democratic, and laissez-faire.[4] Lewin's study was the first of many to show how group behavior adapts to the qualities of the leader. When a leader is authoritarian, commanding team members on what to do, the group adopts the same style. The same was true of democratic and laissez-faire styles.

Lewin's findings concluded that democratic leadership was the most effective because it inspired more cooperation and enjoyment. "Democratic leaders offer guidance to group members, but they also participate in the group and allow input from other group members... Group members feel engaged in the process and are more motivated and creative."[5]

Leaders must be the first to set a growth-minded precedent for a group. And that is what shapes the environment for dreams to be made. It's the first mechanism in launching dream-planning conversations.

Inside of that there's one more shift that needs to happen. People must embrace a "dreams mindset." It's the second prerequisite a culture must have in place before launching into the dream-planning process. You'll learn that next.

CHAPTER 2

EMBRACING A DREAMS MINDSET

"WHAT ARE YOU GOING to dream about tonight?" I asked my daughter Elin, who is five. We have this nightly routine, where I ask her that question after reading one of her favorite books and I tuck her in. My youngest daughter, Izzi, is three. I have the same ritual with her; she just copies her sister at this point.

In our home, it's probably no surprise to you already that Elin and Izzi hear their mom and dad talk about dreams a lot, though right now, for them, dreams only happen at night. They are vivid scenes that play on the projection screen of their minds after their eyes close and their heads hit the pillow. To get them to think happy thoughts before bed I also ask: "what are the only things you're allowed to dream about tonight?"

Then, Elin runs through lists of all the people, places, and stuffed animal buddies that she loves. And she always includes "horses!" Sometimes mermaids. Or, she'll say the names of her grandparents or a favorite babysitter.

Every night, it's pretty much the same. Basically, at this age, my daughter's persistent dreams are the same as Brookelynn's (her mom), which is to acquire as many horses as possible. Ha! During the day when we talk about our aspirations, Brookelynn will say, "Babe, this is the type of stable we need," while pointing to the latest collection of images on her Pinterest board. Working to fulfill each other's dreams is an awesome part of our marriage. (I'll dive into involving partners in dreams a bit more later.)

Whether it's horses today, or princess goals tomorrow, or a dream to buy an entire stable of ponies, I love hearing my girls talk about the myriad of endless possibilities.

Their youth gives them an automatic anything-is-possible attitude. They have no idea at this point that their unicorn dreams aren't entirely doable. They haven't been told over and over to be realistic, like most adults have.

But I also know as they grow, they'll become more pragmatic. Don't get me wrong, practical thinking matters, and they should do that too. But given that my mission is to encourage others to live their dreams, I am adamant that my girls think boldly about what they want and have the support to go after whatever that is, no matter their age.

I'm sure you'd agree that very rarely after you reach a certain age does anybody ask, "What are your dreams?... Your aspirations? ...What's possible?" Most people don't have anyone in their corner encouraging risk-taking, thinking big, or helping them ask "why not?" as they grow.

Most parents indulge in dream thinking until a kid reaches a middling age in their childhood. Then the cold reality of adolescence kicks in. Parents begin to encourage the more rational "we need to be realistic" thinking. Most parents do this because they want the best for their kids. And the best often equates to a higher education, a loving partner, a home, and a secure, well-paying job at XYZ Inc.

Parents need to play this role too. A kid's brain doesn't fully develop until it's twenty-five, so mastering good judgment before then is a physiological impossibility.[6] But this is also why adults can be overly rational since an adult brain works differently than an adolescent brain.

Adults mostly use the rational part of the brain, the prefrontal cortex, for decision-making. Kids think with their amygdala (the brain's emotional center), because the neural connections to their prefrontal cortex are still developing. That's why kids feel more than they think.

There is nothing wrong with a bit of realism. It is useful and important sometimes too. And it usually comes from a good place of wanting what's best for a growing child. No parent wants to see their child struggle, so the advice usually steers them toward investing in their 401k and away from buying a guitar or drum kit or running off to become an actor. Dream thinking can be viewed as the opposite of this type of realistic thinking.

Now, some people do develop a resiliency that lets them buck conventions and not care what their teacher says or what mom and dad think. They follow their instincts and indulge in their aspirations. But most don't. Dream thinking tends to get beaten out of people by the status quo, though I'm sure you'd agree that most people want to be happy. Parental guidance is heavily factored into figuring that out. That makes it fairly common for young people to toss out unconventional aspirations that don't align with the family's assertions for success.

Inspired to start a business selling handmade jewelry? If mom and dad never had any entrepreneurial notions then that idea will be discouraged as too risky, or not practical, or destined to fail. Or possibly, mom and dad attempted entrepreneurship once a long time ago and it didn't succeed. How are you going to pay for a house if you're a struggling jewelry artist, honey?

A parent might point them in another direction, jackhammering a more "practical" idea. You're really great with computers, you should do IT.

A person who hears this enough from an authority figure that they trust, and love, is likely to fire up Google and start looking for entry-level IT jobs, or find a great IT school. I'm willing to bet that conversations like this happen more often than not.

The obsession with making pretty, sparkly things gets replaced with a persuasive self-talk of "Uh, yeah, I'll be a computer engineer. They make good money and it's a pretty secure job." No offense if you are in IT and you love it. For some people, a steady, well-paying job with great benefits is a dream. Nothing wrong with that. But replace jewelry artisan with any dream, and IT job with a so-called realistic well-paying role—lawyer, accountant, working in your father's dry cleaning business—and this story rings true for many people.

Now, when I speak about dreams, they don't need to be as massive as changing careers; that's the beauty of it. They can be smaller things, like learning a new skill or traveling to a new place. The magic in a program like this is that when people start accomplishing even the smallest dreams it invigorates them. They are more excited about their futures. They feel more joyful, playful, and inspired. Many people realize they haven't quite felt this energized with life in a long time, usually since they were a kid.

Following the rational path can be smart and, as a linear route to a decent life, often will result in moderate happiness. That said, it often leads to a different experience of life than waking up every morning and acting on an inspired, unconventional, usually more authentically self-expressed path.

DREAMS MINDSET IS AN EXTENSION OF GROWTH MINDSET

Recall from Chapter 1 that a growth mindset, in its simplest form, is the capacity to ask "What if?" Many workplaces are rational, rigid, and systemized. If they have a culture of rules and limited thinking, a growth mindset may not be encouraged. Asking "What if?" or "How can we?" is the place to start.

In those cases, it takes effort to introduce a growth mindset and change the work culture so the team can start to leverage wonder and consider what's possible in all aspects of their jobs and interactions in the company. Once people ground themselves in the tenets of a growth mindset, they become **seekers instead of acceptors**.

So if a growth mindset asks "What if?" or "How can we?," what is dreams mindset, you might wonder.

Dreams are destinations.

A growth mindset is great to have but a dreams mindset offers a **destination** for growth. Often people will think "What if?" or

"How?" questions, so they think abundantly, but they don't have clear or personalized targets to work toward.

Before I started dream planning I would chase the next promotion, and then think, now what? Then, I would chase the next sales goal. Now what? I always had some goal that I would eventually achieve, and then, it ended with a now what?

I knew I should be growing but I didn't really know why. The dreams mindset gave me a meaningful destination, and an ongoing one too. Later when you learn the dreamstorming process of the book, you'll see that a person will typically create a list of about 200–300 dreams. So there is always another dream on deck once one gets checked off the list. Dreams mindset gives people consistency. It also makes the targets less generic and more meaningful to them. Dreams connect to values, beliefs, and a person's why. The beauty of someone's list is that it's theirs, they created it.

Let's use a tangible example to show how dreams mindset is different from simple goal-setting.

Now, for most people, one of the easiest times to stick to a health goal is when they get engaged and set a wedding date. Once the venue is booked or the invites go out, a bride or groom will have such a concrete vision of what they want, the dream day, that the work they need to do right away is tackled with zeal. It's also often easier to stick to a regimen. Most people think about their wedding day all their life. As soon as it's close, they get excited and they know that the photos are going to live forever. Workouts become a must.

It's also true that for many people, once they get married the health regimen ends. Wedding is over. What's the next thing?

Dreams mindset gives a person a continual purpose because there is always another dream on the list. Once one dream is achieved it usually fires them up to want more. And sometimes there's a compounding effect with dreams where one builds on the next.

I learned how important dreams mindset is as an extension of growth mindset when I hit the worst sales plateau I've ever experienced in 2010. This was long after the Kelly talk where I realized I hadn't been taking much action to forward my personal and professional growth.

You'll recall this from the Introduction. This was when revenues plateaued and my usual strategy of grinding harder was no longer an effective way to produce results.

It's really easy and comfortable for a person to stay in the world of insights and think they are getting somewhere. I did that for a long time. My company is growth-minded. I figured it was enough. The culture I was part of bombarded me with messages on mission and opportunities to attend personal growth seminars and training workshops. It wasn't until 2010 that I learned how I listened more than I took action.

I guess you could say I was a bit of an insight addict. It's easy to fall into this pattern of learning and experience a partial or synthetic form of growth where you think you're growing but you're not. Expanding the mind doesn't mean amplifying the results. In other words, you are ideating a lot, which gives you the notion you are getting somewhere, but really it's in doing, that ideas become reality.

That's how dreams mindset fits in with growth. Learning a new technique, tool, or tactic is the beginning of growing in a new direction. Creating a dream makes that growth automatically more meaningful. And so, dream thinking is the catalyst that makes abstract concepts and growth ideas more personal, and helps mobilize a person to take action.

Dreams are powerful structures that facilitate the follow-through too. They support the action component of a growth mindset. This is why a dreams mindset is critical. It's the mentality of embracing this type of thinking, which is needed to increase the odds of making dreams happen.

Growth mindset and dreams mindset also have a reciprocal relationship. When a person makes a conceptual idea real for themselves by dreaming about it they are more likely to spring into action and make it happen. And then, when a dream comes true, they are more likely to continue to want to grow.

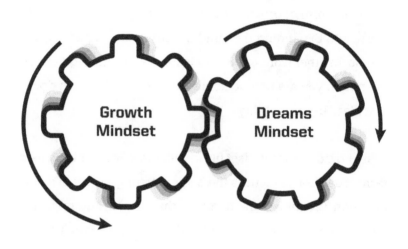

For instance, let's say I engage in a growth mindset by considering, what if I was in the best physical shape of my life? I might extend my thinking by dreaming about how I could get there. Well, I could start by running a marathon because if I could do that by the end of the year, I'd be closer to the best shape of my life. By making it real with a dream it becomes more possible. Then, let's say I take action and book a marathon and start getting up at 5:00 a.m. every day. At the end of the year, I cross the finish line. I completed the dream. I'm more likely to go back to my dreams list and choose another one to pursue.

This is also why in this book and at work, I use the word "dream" intentionally.

THE NUTS AND BOLTS OF BUILDING A DREAMS MINDSET

Now, some might think dreaming is an innate skill and believe that no one needs guidance from a book about that. I'd say, that's not the case. In the last chapter, I talked about implementing a growth mindset in a work culture. Introducing a dreams mindset is what comes next for anyone who plans to bring dream thinking to work.

Just as there are tangible steps to take to build a growth mindset at work, there are also specific actions to encourage a dreams mindset. There are two practices to deploy:

1. Use the word "dream" with intention.

2. Get people to value thinking big.

Let's get into the specifics so that you can start to take it into your workplace. It starts with clarity around the word dream itself.

#1: Use the Word "Dream" With Intention

The concept of dreams, dreaming, and dreams mindset may seem like a weird approach to bring into a business. After all, ask anyone about dreaming and they don't equate it with profit and loss statements, staff retention rates, stock market valuations, and earnest, starched-white discussions about Earnings Before Interest, Taxes, Depreciation and Amortization (EBITDA).

Most people think of a dream as something that's never going to happen. Walk up to anyone and ask them to say three things that come to mind when you say the word "dream" and they may talk about ethereal possibilities, misty future achievements, and for the more practically minded perhaps someday tangibles like a beachfront home, a suitcase of strapped $100 bills, or a toilet made of gold.

The language of dreams conjures up unfulfilled bucket lists or wish lists. There is nothing wrong with a list of things you want. And there is something extraordinarily thrilling about a fulfilled dream, whether it is a personal one or something that would be amazing to fulfill at work.

I wouldn't be surprised if some people rolled their eyes when they first saw this book before they read the description and picked it up. Maybe even you did too. Dreams at work? Huh?

When you start to bring dreaming language into the workplace, you might get that kind of resistance from a few of the more skeptical people on your team. That is okay. They will come around.

What you'll need to do is start to use the word "dream" intentionally at work, before bringing a team together to do the actual dream work. Place value in the word. Get serious about it.

To be practical about it, use the term "dream" as a tangible achievable outcome that fulfills a person's want or need that may have otherwise seemed difficult, unlikely, or even impossible.

You know you are in solid dream territory if the first thought after conceiving the dream is that it would be amazing, but you can't imagine how it would ever happen or come to be because of a reason or series of reasons. The rational mind is the gatekeeper to dreams. When you see it show up and then actively choose to dismiss the rational-mindedness it brings, you know you're in dreams territory.

Let's contextualize how to use it most effectively. I'll also delve deeper into what it is not.

A Dream Goes Beyond a Goal

First, let's distinguish between a dream and a goal. All too often when we set goals they are too small; the bar for success is set too low. Goals aren't particularly inspiring. They don't propel people into action. Simply thinking about a goal usually doesn't put a person in a state of: "Wow, I need to get moving on this now."

I've been helping people set goals in the sales world for a very long time, and I can't begin to tell you how often someone sets a goal that is far beneath their true capability. Often, people will set low goals because they want to ensure they hit them. This is understandable.

What many people don't understand is that the true purpose of goals is not hitting the goal, but who you become in the process. Using the word "dream" allows people to be more comfortable with setting a stretch goal, a number that is far-reaching. It gives more freedom to miss without feeling bad.

A dream is more than a goal. It's an expansion of it. Imagining a dream being achieved is often so inspiring that people want to jump on it immediately. Here's a simple way to distinguish between goal and dream: if a person believes they can achieve a target, they are operating within the confines of a structure of what's possible, and that's a goal.

This Is Not About a Bucket List

Using the word "dream" intentionally also helps to separate it from the type of dream a person would write on a bucket list. Those types of dreams are usually "I'll get to it when I retire" ideas. They are someday phenomena. This is not about a bucket list that a person may or may not get to. Using the word "dream" intentionally is meant to get somebody out of their own head, out of their realm of what's possible, to think in an entirely different way. This is especially useful at work.

Dreaming Is a Skill Lost to Childhood

Use the word "dream" simply because we all recognize and know how to do it, at least on a conceptual level. Kids are great dreamers. Dreaming is hardwired into us from childhood, even if we reject the notion as we grow into rational-thinking adults. If I were to ask ten adults for one hundred dreams that are attainable in their life, it is unlikely that many—if any—of them would be able to do it. Ask ten children and there is significantly less resistance. You'll get answers like: I would have a pet dinosaur. I would eat a whole room of ice cream. I would be a mermaid and hang out with the fish. I would be a flying sparkly unicorn (that's the most common one in my house right now).

Adults tend to be less fanciful and certainly less inspiring, at first. Again, goals are targets people know they can achieve. If

Jessica in accounts payable told you she wanted to be a mermaid and hang out with the fish, you might wonder about her mental health.

The good news is that by using the word "dream" a person is immediately launched into an expanded level of thinking.

The act of dreaming means to put everything aside...ignore financial constraints, current work situations, physical shape. That, as well as the ability to breathe underwater and grow a fishtail, as in Jessica's case.

Abandon rationality and instead ask:

- What would be fun?

- What would be exciting?

- What would light me up?

A dreams mindset requires that a person venture away from what might be their default thinking of being realistic, or practical, or taking the safe path. None of those are inspiring. It's too easy for us to base our goals off our current situation or a slight increase of lifestyle. It's difficult for us to set a goal that is significantly different from our current life. The value of a dreams mindset is getting someone to unlock massive shifts in life by starting with an unbounded style of thinking.

#2: Get People to Value Thinking Big

The dreams mindset makes thinking big possible, and there's serious value in thinking big in the workplace. When people understand why thinking big is practical and important they are more likely to do it. Raise the following arguments to dream naysayers. They'll no longer be able to dispute that a dreams mindset is a practice they should embrace.

Workplace Innovators Are Dreamers

A dreams mindset creates a container for big thinkers. And, the world and workplace need big thinkers more than ever because they are innovation drivers. They are the Steve Jobs and Elon Musks of the world. The ones who create remarkable businesses that revolutionize the way we live and move the world forward. The willingness to dream big and fearlessly is the way massive ideas are launched and lived.

Yet, I've seen people resist a basic two-day Dreams Retreat if they've never done it because they feel it's a waste of time. That type of person will probably not drill and build underground highways across Los Angeles, as Musk's The Boring Company is planning to do. (By the way, how perfect is that name for Musk's company?)

Big Thinkers Solve Big Problems

Thinking big is more important in business today than it's ever been. The business landscape of today is one of disruption. Companies are being broadsided by many different factors that are shaking our industries, altering marketing, and decimating long-established rules. A company used to edge ahead of its competition with better pricing, smarter branding, location strategy. That's not the case anymore.

In 2020, the COVID-19 pandemic, an infectious disease that spread across the globe, shut down businesses everywhere. People had to suddenly leave the office and work from home.

Dreams give people purpose. They keep them moving forward during tough times. They keep morale high. And even more, big thinking is desperately needed. When threats emerge out of nowhere, team members need to adapt fast. Three months into the pandemic I reached out to a top sales performer on our team, Robert Wicks. Bert had been working with us for many years and had a fully developed dreams list. He works on our Events Program, which means he sells Cutco at fairs, expos, and a variety of in-person events. I'm sure you could imagine that his personal business was negatively impacted by COVID.

I reached out to see how he was holding up. I was expecting a tough phone call. Bert sounded cheerful and said, "I've accomplished more on my dreams list than any other stretch of time. I even just completed flossing for thirty days straight!" Haha, I had no idea that flossing made the dreams list.

A massive inspiring vision is one way to amass team members and keep a culture thriving. Naveen Jain, author of the book *Moonshots: Creating a World of Abundance*,[7] wrote: "The only truly scarce resources in this world are imagination, curiosity, and creativity."

Jain explains that the bigger and crazier an idea is, the easier it is to execute because people want to get behind it. And Jain has certainly done this with his company, Viome. The company's mission is to eradicate disease by providing health intelligence products that assess gut microbiome, cellular health, mitochondrial health, immune system health, and stress response, and suggest diet solutions linked to a person's DNA.

Jain's wild mission to "eradicate disease" allowed him to link up to the most brilliant scientists in the world. Simply by hearing his mission they wanted to join him because the idea itself is incredibly inspiring and worth dedicating a career to.

Dreams move people beyond natural ceilings. At work and in the world we need more people who dream and aren't willing to settle for anything less. As I am writing this book, I just interviewed a nineteen-year-old who embraced the type of refreshing thinking that's so important today in business.

"I want to be a music teacher, but I know I can't make the money doing that yet, so I'm also learning real estate," she said. "I figured if I buy some properties, I can have the financial stability to be a music teacher too."

That "how" type of thinking is awesome.

When a person experiences a roadblock but goes beyond it by getting curious, they can easily find solutions. So many people are held back because they've been conditioned to be overly realistic. They might think because this is the job path they chose, they can't pivot to another career. Or because a dream they want costs money, there's no way it can happen.

Again, COVID-19 is such a great example of why the dreams mindset is so important in business today. Companies had these notions that too many workers online would make it impossible to run a business. Then they were forced to. Schools had to move online too. For many, it improved the lifestyle of employees but never would have happened if they didn't adapt and ask "how?"

When people don't consider that there is any way to make an "impossible" goal happen, they stop themselves from ever achieving it right then and there. Dreams mindset, and asking how, is the way to get around it.

Dreams Motivate Us to Take Action

In 2016, Brookelynn and I had our first child and I took five weeks off to be with my family. I'd never taken this much time off before but I knew that this was a special time for us and I wanted to be as present as possible.

There were many evenings where I'd wake up because Brookelynn was up for late-night feedings. When the baby was fed I'd take her in my arms and rock her back to sleep. Many of these nights, I'd sit and stare at the precious bundle in my arms. My mind would be absorbed in the moment with thoughts of gratitude and then it would wander to other ideas.

Though I was home and loving my first days of being a father, I still thought a lot about business. I also found that during that time I birthed many new thrilling ideas. When I went back after my five-week leave I had a new approach. I put big ideas into action and that next year, our business grew 70 percent.

I've since learned that there's a scientific reason for why people get great ideas when they are doing nothing. If you've ever had the experience of getting brilliant ideas when you're in the shower, on your commute to work, or while lying on a chair with its feet dug in the sand with a coconut in your hand watching your kids and wife jump through waves on a beach in Cancun, there's scientific evidence to show this makes sense.

This phenomenon is credited to two neural networks in the brain: default mode network (DMN) and task positive network (TPN).[8] DMN takes over when the brain isn't focused on something specific, like "attending to a physical activity, interacting with the world around you, or involved in dialogue." On the other hand, the brain switches to TPN for tasks that are demanding of its full attention. Creativity (and those ideas you come up with in the shower) has been linked to areas of the DMN and "may also involve uncontrolled processes."[9]

It's not bad to get curious. To ask how. To question ideas. And when you do, you get better answers.

When a person gets specific about their personal dreams, a way to grow becomes more real.

The idea of personal growth was exciting to me but it didn't have a defined endpoint; it didn't have a specific outcome that inspired me. Of course I wanted to grow and achieve more, but once I got clear on my dreams there was purpose behind the personal growth.

Before I used dream language in my organization, the collective conversation was, "Hey, you should grow personally and here's how it's going to impact your business." And not "what dreams do you want to achieve?"

HOW TO BRING DREAMS MINDSET TO EVERYDAY WORK CONVERSATIONS

B efore you lead any dream workshop, you want your team members to be on board—or at least curious—with the idea. To that end, create the right atmosphere for team members to start dreaming about themselves. Begin by engaging your team in "how" questioning. Don't stop at "what would be cool?" Ask, "Okay, how could we make that really happen?" When people think this way they get excited and feel compelled to take action. This subtle tweak to conversations makes a massive difference.

Living your own dreams out loud, no matter your status in the company, helps expand the thinking of those around you. People easily fall into a rhythm in life of doing the same thing they did last year over and over again, and never really being fulfilled. They will naturally begin dreaming more if you lead by example.

Many people in leadership roles are tight-lipped about the life they live. It's normal for someone in a leadership role to be quiet about a great vacation they took with their family, possibly because they know that trip wouldn't be an option for others at work due to financial constraints. They also may simply prefer to keep their private life private. They may not want to be super vocal about a vacation because they worry their employees will think they're bragging.

But a leader's dreams should be shared with enthusiasm and authenticity. When they are shown, they inspire others to dream too. When the dream culture is thriving, people support it and they're fired up about it. It's important to acknowledge: "Hey, we all, including myself, are trying to live the life of our dreams." Opening the dialogue of dreams in a culture acknowledges this, makes it central, and creates a bonded team where everyone is rooting for each other.

With a growth mindset and a willingness to dream, any leader can successfully help their people think this way. These are the best conditions for bringing a dream-planning process to a company.

By now you should have a solid grounding in the concept of a dreams mindset and its relationship with a growth mindset. I've covered the initial strategies of introducing it into your workplace and provided some tactics on how to do that.

Still, there is more you need to know to be able to follow through. In the next chapter I am going to train you in how to design and launch what I call a Dreams Retreat. These events are the workhorse of the philosophy. It's where people put the dream technology into action for themselves, both at home and in the office. The Dreams Retreat is the key structure that gives a team time and guidance to do the dream-planning work.

CHAPTER 3

THE DREAMS RETREAT

"SCRAP IT. WE'RE NOT going to talk about work at all this year," I said. It was a bit of a risky idea but the leadership team agreed. "Okay, we're aligned. This year, it's 100 percent dreams," they said.

I was thankful. It was time to do something different.

Every August our organization has a sales and management conference that consists of an overnight stay in a nice hotel in a large city in the US. In August 2017, my division replaced our typical leadership event with our first ever Dreams Retreat. We replaced the hotel with a summer camp style resort in a small town a few hours outside of Minneapolis. This was done purposefully to separate the experience from work and make it about the people and not the company and make the distinction that this was a different event.

For my company, our business cycle ends at the end of the normal calendar year. But for my division, we hold an event at the end of August. We do this primarily to engage our most talented people and demonstrate to them that they matter to the organization. This critical meeting is an opportunity to sell our high performers on the idea of staying with the organization for the next twelve months. Top-performing salespeople are often on the lookout for the next, potentially better, opportunity—that sometimes happens to be at another company.

So that year we skipped the usual presentations and graph-driven company performance reviews. We also dumped the standard awards event where exceptional team talent comes up onto the stage to collect faux-crystal professional development awards. We abandoned the stuffy business attire too. We wanted it to be about them. We wanted to see what would happen if the leadership team went all-in on the dreams concept.

Prior to this, we were less structured about dreams at work. For four years, I would typically lead a half-day workshop each year that reinforced the concept and was always well received. Some people embraced it. They ran with what they learned, creating new dreams lists, checking off previous years' dreams achieved, and celebrating them with their peers.

We noticed that the dreams workshop enthusiasts also upped their game at work. So, the leadership team agreed expanding the program into a retreat would be a great experiment that drove home the dreams process. We were curious to learn if it would produce bigger results, improve staff retention, and impact company performance as I believed it would—I'd seen it for myself and my team.

As we saw with the science mentioned before, people often also get their best ideas outside of work. Dream thinking comes more readily while on a hike, biking a trail, or wandering along the waterline of a picturesque beach. Maybe you have a special spot in your house where you sink into a chair and get your best ideas. Or maybe you dream best when you're under a spray of warm water in the shower or as your mind wanders during your commute to work while a rocking tune blares from the car stereo.

Now, while you might have great ideas at work, usually they are job-centric ideas. My point is that dreaming is easiest when a person is in a relaxed, inspired state. Dreams often hit us when we least expect it, and the best places for stimulating dreams are safe, relaxed, aesthetically arousing environments.

For our retreat, we hypothesized that if the event was solely about dreams and excluded work content, the experience would be further enhanced for our team. People would have the time to dive deep into the thinking work required to plan and execute on dreams.

As a side effect, bonds between team members would grow strong. In turn, a deeper affinity between participants and the company would develop, making a rise in retention seem like a given result.

To get people to do the actual work of dream planning, and do it effectively, time needs to be set aside to actually do the work. By iterating on the event over the years, I've learned there's a specific way to do the work successfully. Like most systems, mine started smaller and then I developed it over time, making adjustments to improve the outcomes.

This three-phase process is the most effective approach:

- **Stage 1—Dreamstorming:** Where the brainstorming of dreams happens. We break life down into nine categories and build dream lists.

- **Stage 2—Dream Sharing & Stealing:** The first step to making a dream real is vocalizing it. When a dream goes from head to expressed desire it becomes real for a person, or helps them achieve their dreams by sharing resources or teaming up. So dream sharing is a critical second step. During this second stage, as team members share, people also get to dream steal when they get inspired by someone else's wild ideas. This section leads to some great bonds forming amongst a team.

- **Stage 3—Dream Planning:** Dreams don't happen unless a person takes action. So in this third stage, a person focuses on the actions they can take immediately to make their dreams come true.

If you skip one of these crucial steps, there's a predictable outcome: any dreams created by the participants remain just dreams. In other words, they tend not to be realized.

So to launch the dreams concept successfully for any work group, the best method is the Dreams Retreat that follows this three-step process.

While it's possible to do all three phases in a one-day workshop, it's most effective when delivered with ample workshop time and downtime in between. We have found that the conversations team members have during this event are really valuable. They further relationships and have space to engage in conversation that centers on their personal lives.

Each step contains valuable nuances and actions that help effectively train participants in the dreams concept. In the next few chapters you'll learn the intricacies of the process so you can launch a Dreams Retreat at your company. Before that, it's necessary to conceptually understand the strategy behind it all.

WHY A DREAMS
RETREAT?

D reams have given my division the ability to attract, inspire, and engage the sales stars, retain the moderate performers, and shape the juniors into brilliant future leaders.

I knew the dreams concept would work long before I brought it to my team. Early on, creating dream lists was a personal process. Then when my wife joined, I knew it worked better with more than one person. But still, I wasn't sure how to introduce it at work. Would I lead a workshop? Who would be included? Start small and expand from there? That all made sense.

The first phase was experimental. I brought my dream list idea to a small group of managers in my division. I held a two-hour workshop and shared my process and results. I walked them through a basic brainstorming session and a list-creation exercise. The mandate was: "everybody needs at the very least to create a list." That's how it started.

It was less of a mandate, though, and more of a suggestion at this point. Once the managers did it, I encouraged them to do the same exercise with their teams, and then put together a dreams board in their office to celebrate wins.

The idea was that if the leaders in each organization were achieving their dreams, shared about it, and used more dreams language, their teams would be intrigued and more likely to want to stick around and advance so they could experience the same.

Do you recall the graph from 2013 in this book's Introduction? That was the year this process was put into play. It was the first time we experienced a big bump in our bottom line.

It was obvious that the dream workshop with my managers had had an effect. So from 2013 to 2016, we deployed a two-hour workshop cycle. This was version 1.0. We would help people create their dreams lists and then we would recognize the accomplishments in our respective offices.

Any manager who had been with us for more than one year had a dreams list, though at this point we still had not rolled the process out to everybody in the organization. But a cultural dialogue emerged. People talked about achieving their dreams. And there was a dream vibe across the division. It was quite amazing. But still, the process was imperfect. So I worked to customize it, systemize it, and fully install it as a key part of our work culture.

The dream concept was valued differently from person to person. Some teammates made their list and said "this is great," and ran with it. Once somebody creates their list, that's the bulk of the work, though what's more important is that they identify and take actions to make those dreams come true. There were inconsistencies with follow-through in my initial model.

At this point, we gave them the structure and training to create a dreams list. However, if they did nothing with it beyond that, that was their prerogative.

I noticed that if a person made even one dream happen, they became addicted to the concept and wanted to do more. I knew I had to refine the process to build more buzz around it and ignite more action.

The second revelation I had about dream planning at work was that it worked better when done in teams. For me, when I brought it to my wife, we held each other accountable and built on the dreams we conjured up together. That amplified the excitement and inspired us to commit to dream-realizing actions.

Having more than one person on board creates an immediate accountability structure. You sit and create a dreams list because you have a dreams cheerleader there to inspire you, collaborate with you, and celebrate with you when you succeed. And so, dream planning with a team helped ensure that it got done for everyone.

For most people, creating a dreams list on their own is just not going to go well. It's not that somebody can't come up with ideas on their own. It's more about the environment and accountability and the fact that someone else is leading you through exercises. The participant is also watching everyone else participate full out. It allows you to be wholly present and immersed in the process. The full-day workshop and my second iteration, the Dreams Retreat, worked even better than the two-hour workshop version. Immersion in the process and separation from distractions are key.

When was the last time you sat down and wrote a dream list? For most people, the answer is never. It's simply not a structure anyone generally uses or even knows to use. So, initiating a workshop or event or carving out time to do the dream work puts a process in place that is bracketed by time constraints, which enables focused activities.

These were the reasons we revamped our dreams workshop process and spun it into a longer Dreams Retreat. To begin, we invited seven of my managers and their spouses to a holiday party. We rented a large historic mansion in Minneapolis so everyone could fully participate. The event began with a great dinner, drinks, and socializing. Then the next morning we ran a session where I coached everyone—managers and spouses—to create a dreams list.

I was nervous about the spouses because they had not been exposed to the dreams concept that we use at work. I believed in the concept but was uncertain if they'd engage fully with the list. Along with the usual dreamstorming process and list creation, I added two additional steps: dream sharing and dream planning. Those have proved to be critical iterations, which we'll explore in detail shortly.

The overnight was an epic success. The spouses were open to the process and participated the same as anyone within our organization. The powerful part was watching spouses share their dreams with each other.

The feedback I received from our seven leaders was phenomenal. I knew we had something. Their spouses really became involved in the process. They now understood why my team members valued our team and were excited about our culture.

Given the success of the event for managers and spouses, we replicated it with the entire team, and the results were epic.

ELEMENTS OF AN EFFECTIVE DREAMS RETREAT

Before we get to the workflow, let me share a few more pointers on making your Dreams Retreat effective.

It's not only about the phases of work, it's also about the environment you create. Creating an atmosphere that's conducive to thinking about dreams is critical to the success of any Dreams Retreat. Here are guidelines to stick to:

1. Escape the daily work digs.

2. Don't talk about work.

3. Invite partners if possible.

4. Iterate.

These basic foundational atmospheric elements of a Dreams Retreat contribute to setting everyone up to win and shouldn't be overlooked or taken for granted.

Escape the Daily Work Digs

People need to feel safe so they are free to dream. It's probably why, as you learned in Chapter 2, people get their best ideas when they aren't focused on a task. When the mind is free to wander, it fills up with enchanting thoughts of what could be.

A strategically chosen environment helps to encourage these states of feeling safe, relaxed, and open-minded. So get out of the office, if it's possible.

The last in-person Dreams Retreat we held before the COVID-19 pandemic turned work life upside down was held at a retreat facility. The brainstorming, planning, and all the group work was done in the large great room. But in between each of the stages of the entire Dreams Retreat process everyone ventured outside. We had barbecues. We played games. We hung out and talked about our families and hobbies and life outside of work.

The in-out movement of the group was intentional. It primed people for deep-work, dream planning time balanced with hours of play with peers to give their brains a break.

While dream work is meant to be fun and joyful, it also takes some deep introspection. Sitting inside doing dream work all day shouldn't feel so mentally taxing that it's not fun anymore.

Be sure to mix up the atmosphere to create the vibe you want and the mood you want people to feel. Keep it simple. The vibe should alternate between deep work, then relax/play/fun, then deep work followed by more downtime, for each phase.

Keep it casual, especially if you need to do it in an office. You want people to feel comfortable. If you do it at your office, schedule it on a Friday and make it a jeans day. Or, if you're at a retreat center, an exotic locale, or a plush hotel, let people wear what they want. Flip-flops by the pool are not a horrible idea, if people are comfortable in pool wear in front of coworkers. You might want to stop at bikinis and swim shorts, but gauge what is appropriate for the group. In this casual, holiday-like setting, real friendships will form outside of work. You will see a stronger team emerge when everyone is back in the office.

Don't Talk About Work

In the brainstorming process, we talk about vocation. While dreams are tied to work, any other discussions about work should be set aside during a Dreams Retreat. Focus on dreams only. Each person should think about themselves to create their dreams list. They don't need to concentrate on the project on their desk that's due next Wednesday, or talk to their coworkers about just work.

You want the participants to come back from the retreat refreshed, as if they went to a spa for the weekend. And heck, maybe there is a spa at the destination you choose. You could include a massage package as part of the whole deal.

When a person is told by their employer they need to focus on themselves and their dreams, it shows that their employer really cares about them. There's a different level of loyalty that forms. When the conversation is 100 percent about them, they will feel differently about the company. Among your friends and family, you may hear some people harp on their boss and the company they work for because "they don't care about us" or "they don't do anything for us." Those complaints will start to vanish on your team, if they were ever there. Higher levels of performance and dedication become unlocked when a person feels appreciated by the organization they work for.

This process also naturally opens people up to being more transparent and vulnerable. You can't talk about your dreams with someone without letting them into your personal and family life a little. Inevitably, the majority of dreams will be personal—and they should be—although there may be some work dreams on the list too. For some it may be to start their own business someday. For others, it may be to rise to senior management. For a junior it may be to become a sales star or be promoted to a specialty role. Dreams like those often pepper some people's lists.

Invite Partners If Possible

Remember how my wife, Brookelynn, and my two very cute little girls have a horse obsession?

Well, let me just say it really helps to have a partner who is in on the whole dream list lifestyle. I support Brookelynn and she supports me. We have a back-and-forth dialogue about how to make dreams happen and we work through ideas when we're not on the same page. We both bring dreams to each other and are willing to come to the table and figure out how to support each other to reach them. Brookelynn is somewhat ingenuous about the horse dreams.

"Just because it's on your dream list doesn't mean it's happening. That's not how it works," I say to Brookelynn sometimes when she comes to me all doe-eyed with a showcase of images on her tablet of the luxury horse stalls. I'm joking of course. We are serious about supporting each other. Anything is possible. But dreams often take a team and certainly they need partner support.

After Brookelynn watches videos on luxury stables she sometimes comes to me with a pitch. "So I just really feel like we need to buy this land in Sedona and build a stable."

I might have to reel her in a bit. The land may not be for sale. And it may not fit with the current household budget. I test to see if it is whimsy or if she is super serious about the idea. If she is, we add it to the list and we figure out how to make it happen.

Not everything on a dreams list is immediate, but if it's serious, anything is achievable. The buy-in of a spouse or partner to the dreams concept helps make any dreams a reality. For instance, this book was a dream I brought to Brookelynn. The project requires a significant investment of my time and our resources. The green light she gave me, and her dedication to this book too, was a critical component of it coming to fruition. In my opinion, life becomes more fun when you and your partner are aligned and pursuing your dreams.

Sometimes one person's dream is another person's nightmare. A middle-aged man that scuba dived in the Maldives in his youth may want to take it up again now that he is married. Of course, that would require him to recruit his wife to get scuba-trained and take the plunge. If she is fish phobic, or not a confident swimmer, it may not be an easy sell. Still, all dreams are negotiable. She may decline swimming with reef sharks and all manner of sea critters, but she could still support an annual trip and take up a relaxing post by the hotel infinity pool while her husband boards the dive boat each morning.

It's really important that partners and family understand the dreams process, because living a declared dream usually involves family finances and participation. It's nice when a spouse gets excited about a dream their partner has and doesn't spike it into the ground on account of, say, her fear of sharks.

Suddenly bringing a dream plan home from work to an uninitiated spouse may not always go well, at least not without a little forethought. So if somebody comes home from work and is like, "I have this dreams list that I made," the response may be, "Wait, what?" How do you navigate a possible dreams gap?

When we included spouses in the dreams retreat, it was very well received. The spouse can be a lynchpin in making dreams happen.

That was the case for Connor and his wife, Kelsey. In 2017, at our annual Dreams Retreat with partners, they wrote on their lists: "have our dream wedding at a castle in Ireland." One year later, I was there with them. I was invited to become the officiant and married them too. Their wedding was a spectacular moment for us all. They were married at Bellinter House, a luxurious eighteenth century Georgian manor on the banks of the River Boyne, just outside of Dublin. The venue was the kind you'd see in a historic film or a Netflix series. It was an estate that would fit well in a scene of a show like *Downton Abbey*, except with more rolling green hills.

Also, as the support person, a spouse doesn't necessarily have a window into what is going on at work for their partner. So it's amazing to also offer an inspiring dreams process like this to them too. Sometimes the spouses are more enthusiastic about the dreams process than the employees. A few I've involved have taken it on with a surprising amount of zeal, showing up as leaders in the process. A member on my team named Marie brought her husband, Chris, to a Dreams Retreat. He was a little uncertain at first. By the time we were done with the sharing, Chris had built his list well over one hundred. That next year he accomplished three things on his dreams list and the following year he accomplished sixteen!

Iterate

Introducing the dreams process in phases is most effective. The process should start with you, grow to a small group, then expand to the entire team. Depending on current company culture, the process can be expedited or rolled out slowly. But introducing it little by little is the best way to open the dialogue, persuade the team on the value of the process, and make sure the ideas land. It will also give you (or the leader running the program) the chance to adjust to the process and build confidence in what you're doing.

Your rank at your company doesn't matter. You could be the leader of the division, like I was, who brings it to a few managers, who then train their teams.

Or, if you're a middle manager, you could start small and develop dreams lists with your team. Demonstrate your performance and show the company leadership the results.

A junior or new hire can bring it to their leaders or peers too. It's a great way to get noticed, produce results fast, and lead from the ground up. The results you produce will improve your performance, give you an edge, and make you stand out at work.

When you iterate each year on your process, the people you do it with will also help you prove and improve the concept. They may talk differently at work. They will share dream wins. Their personal stories and performance will get noticed by others in the company.

It starts with you as the leader, and you must lead by example for the process to be effective. I will discuss this more in the Conclusion of this book. When a leader dives into the dream mindset, they naturally share their own dream wins. And through that, their team will become more connected to them. Team members will witness the transformation, and they might want it for themselves. They'll also see that the leader is a person who is more than just a colleague or boss. The dreams that you share don't need to be these big flashy things. They can be losing five pounds, running a 10K race, finishing a home project, or getting extra time with family.

The process exposes a person's humanity, that they have aspirations as a parent or spouse, or whoever they are outside of work. Others may also learn that the person isn't where they want to be healthwise. The process requires vulnerability, and that is a carrier to connection, empathy, and relatedness among staff.

Of course, the vulnerability required may terrify some and you will inevitably see resistance from a few players. People hear about dreams planning and can be skeptical. To overcome resistance, a leader must demonstrate the process and show others the power of dreams. If this is successfully done, skepticism will begin to melt away as teammates see their own dreams as possible.

After all, humans are highly self-interested. We all seek pleasure and try to avoid pain. If you show them that they too can have whatever they might dream about, you will start to convert them. As they start to trust the process, you'll be the witness to some amazing turnarounds.

If you set a few dream goals and achieve them, your colleagues won't look upon the process as weird or woo-woo. They will start to see it as a legitimate goal-fulfillment or motivational exercise. It's amazing what can happen if you share your scuba dream and then later that year come back from a holiday in the Florida Keys with underwater pictures of sharks and a smiling scuba-kitted spouse.

Now that you know iteration is key, let's talk about the three steps, starting first with Stage 1—Dreamstorming.

CHAPTER 4

THE DREAMSTORMING PROCESS

WE ARE ABOUT TO embark on stimulating what I call the heartbeat of the The Dream Machine process: dreamstorming. Okay, so let's talk about elephants. What I mean is, I'm going to use an elephant to help illustrate it. But wait, I'm getting ahead of myself. Let's back up.

Dreamstorming is the first critical phase of the Dream Machine process. It's where we get participants to come up with a huge list of dreams that excite them. To make that happen, it's important to induce a state of abundance and fun in each participant. With that mindset, the mission becomes easier. The idea is to get them to write down one hundred or more dreams that reflect what they might want to accomplish in multiple areas of their life.

To do that I used to use verbal "thought joggers," a list of places to visit, aspirational ideas, and wildly awesome accomplishments that prompt participants to conjure up their own dreams. (You can access this master list on my website at www.DaneEspegard. com. It's free.)

But I've found that while verbal joggers are effective, it's even better to use images. The reason is because of how the brain works. To illustrate this, let's get back to elephants.

If you sat in front of me and I said "elephant" to you, what would that make you think of? Well, you would probably imagine a giant gray animal with floppy ears and a trunk. If you have kids, maybe you'd think of the movie *Dumbo* or the bejeweled variety you once saw at a circus. Or you might think that Dane has gone insane, which would also be a reasonable response.

However, if I showed you a picture of a family of elephants bathing in swampy water, with baby ones too, you might smile. Or a picture of elephants eating from troughs of bananas (which I have witnessed when I once visited Chiang Mai, Thailand). You might notice in the picture that the backdrop to the elephants in the scene is a tropical climate. You might then think of the last time you were somewhere warm or tropical, or even on a beach. Or that time you went to the zoo and saw elephants at play.

Notice, however, that the rational mind starts to look for connections to a word. Elephant? Animal. Giant. Dumbo. Why is he talking about elephants?

But presented with an image, you are more likely to have an emotional response: Aww, that's cute. Or maybe situational thoughts might fire: Elephants bathing in the sun. Oh, that looks warm. I love the sun. Oh, it would be nice to visit somewhere warm soon. Maybe Mexico. Hmm. Or memories may flood your brain: I loved when I went to the zoo with my kids when they were little and we saw elephants cavorting in the water.

I've discovered that showing images to the participants versus just using words works wonders to inspire a cascade of dreams they can then write down. That is because the human brain processes visuals faster than it processes the language associated with them.

The human attention span times out after eight seconds, so showing a series of easy-to-process images can help participants kick-start the process. The human brain processes color images in a little over two seconds. To take advantage of this fact, I now use a deck of 500 to 1000 images that I project on a screen.

Now, you don't have to use a picture of an elephant. It's just a silly example. But you could.

My parade of images usually contains a massive set selection of curated images that I have carefully chosen to provoke thought and inspiration. (Find out how to get your hands on the deck on my website too.)

The images are a mix of people, places, and things. There are a good quantity of travel pictures, which always get people fired up. Mixed in might also be images of actual dreams achieved by team members. These cater to even the most practical and scarcity-minded person in the room. I might show Sarah in a set of Lulus sporting a medal around her neck because she completed a half-marathon. Or a picture of Bobby and his wife, Lera, in front of their new custom-built home. Vocation-related photos win hearts too. I show a great image of Jon giving his first speech at a work event, post stage fright of course.

"Before we dive into our dreamstorming session, let me show you what some team members have accomplished since last year's event," I say.

When you open a Dreams Retreat, it's inspiring to share about dreams achieved by other people who have gone through the process previously. If it's the first event and there is no history, the leader should share their own journey.

This sets everyone up for success so they immediately understand the value of the work they're about to engage in. So use verbal thought joggers, or pictures. Videos in a PowerPoint presentation also work wonders. Tell vividly described stories as well.

It's important to create what could be but also to keep it no-pressure. So you paint the picture that in twelve months any one person in the room could be seeing you flip through a collection of their photos because they accomplished ten or more dreams. But also, point out that some people might only check one or two dreams off the list. The idea is for everyone to leave with a heightened level of purpose.

After the introduction where everyone is suitably stimulated and hearts are racing and ideas are flowing, I move on to Stage 1, which is what I call Dreamstorming.

John Ernst Steinbeck Jr. was an American author who wrote: "Ideas are like rabbits. You get a couple and learn how to handle them, and pretty soon you have a dozen." It helps to think of Stage 1—Dreamstorming much like this. It's about catching ideas and adding to them without need for reason. Rational thinking comes later.

During this phase people brainstorm to create dream lists and participants are given free license to engage in wonder. The idea is for participants to set rational thinking aside, no limitation, no money constraints.

Of course, putting practicality aside is not always simple. So this warrants a discussion.

GROUNDWORK
FOR DREAMSTORMING

F raming is a psychological term that defines the process of manipulating the presentation of information to influence and alter decision-making about that information.[10] Basically, it's the difference between looking at the glass half-empty (negative frame) or half-full (positive frame).

Often used in politics via images and words, framing sways how people think about information and communicate about it. So, as I lead a dream workshop I am very deliberate about how I frame ideas and concepts so they land in a way that makes the dreams concept practical.

Live Life by Design

I often open a dreamstorming session by showing these words on a slide. To truly live a life by design a person has to get clear on what that is. This is why dreamstorming is critical.

How often do we say something like "time got away from me" or "I don't know where the time went"? Those aren't typically statements of excitement, more from a place of regret. Living life by design means being intentional with the things I want and taking it a step further to say I will put them into my calendar and take action.

But what does that really look like? Ask most people what they want in life and the answer is usually, "Be happy." Yet each person has a different version in their head of what "be happy" means. One person's life by design could be another's worst nightmare. Some people have never thought about their life by design and have simply fallen into jobs, relationships, apartments—taking the first that comes along without intention. Many people also aren't shown an example of living the way they'd like to live. Therefore, they follow the status quo.

So what does life by design mean to most people? Perhaps it requires more thought than most people give it. And this is where you give people that time.

"What if you took a step forward every year?" I ask the group. "What if every action you took, and all the decisions that you made, lined up with a future—a life by design—you were truly excited about?"

This encourages people not to overthink. The idea is, if it sounds great at that moment then write it down. The list isn't a forever list; they have the ability to revise it whenever they would like to.

It doesn't take long for the entire room to get on board with the idea. Most people dream less as they age. Kids have insanely awesome ideas, and then as they encounter their teens and grow into young adulthood a dreaded realism kicks in.

When I present this to my workshops, people start to see the valid reasons they are there and the opportunity they have been given. When I introduce the dreamstorming concept, I frame it in a very intentional way.

To successfully set the group up to do the dreamstorming work effectively, it's best to follow this format:

- Step 1: Build a connection.

- Step 2: Use leverage.

- Step 3: Set expectations.

Step 1:
Build a Connection

All great salespeople know the first step to selling a product, service, or idea is to create relatability. You have to understand the worldview of the person you're selling to before they will listen to what you have to say.

At Cutco, we're in the business of selling the world's finest knives. Our salespeople never tell a customer they need to buy the Homemaker + 8 Set Block without first knowing if the person has a crappy knife set on their kitchen counter.

There's a specific line of inquiry they engage in: What kind of cooking does your family do? Do you cook because you have to, like to, or love to? Have some of your knives ever gone dull over the years?

When they understand what a buyer thinks, wants, and needs, they can offer support instead of blindly pushing a product on them.

So in a similar way here it's imperative to speak to the needs and wants of the people in the room. In turn they are more likely to be open to what you have to say. The odds of getting them onside with the entire dreams process exponentially increase too.

The leader of a dreamstorming session is obviously sold on the idea. They know dreams have value and the work their group is doing is important. And while some people on your team might agree, there will be people in the room who don't. Some contrarians think that dreams are "fluffy." They won't happen. They are not possible. Or they are impractical and a waste of time. And there's always a middle camp too, that sits in judgment until you win them over, or don't.

The first step is to acknowledge all types of mindsets in the room. Then state your case, using solid fact-based arguments to seek agreement from everybody. This contextualizes the session so everyone gets focused on the work at hand and ensures they get serious about their lists and process.

Not everyone needs to be a total dream fanatic from the get-go, but they must be willing to be open, do the basic work, and make a dream list at the retreat. As a leader, if you've done the work in Chapters 1 and 2 of encouraging a growth mindset and a dreams mindset at the company, you'll increase the likelihood that the group in the room will be open to the process.

I've found two general arguments that work to open the minds of the skeptics or middle-of-the-roaders. Most people will agree with these commonsense arguments.

Dreamstorming Is Surprisingly Practical

Argument 1: Your Future Outlook Inspires Your Now

You saw this quote in this book's Introduction, but I am bringing it back now because it's key:

"When there's hope in the future, there's power in the present."

This idea underpins this entire process. It's the reason for the dreamstorming work in this chapter as well as the two that follow. It's the overarching idea that provides evidence as to why this process works. And there's science to back it up too.

Viktor Frankl was a famous groundbreaking psychologist widely known for his book *Man's Searching for Meaning*. Frankl pioneered logotherapy, a theory founded on the belief that human nature is motivated by the search for a life purpose. In other words, the future a person believes they are headed toward shapes how they feel in the moment.

Frankl was a practicing psychologist and a contemporary of famed psychologist Sigmund Freud. During World War II he was arrested for being Jewish and then sent to a succession of Nazi concentration camps.

During his imprisonment, he studied his fellow prisoners and discovered that the ones who survived tended to believe in a brighter future. Their hopefulness gave them an edge. Some believed they would eventually reconnect with family members. Others turned to their faith, believing that although their circumstances were inhumane, there was a deeper or more divine reason for them.

Having an inspiring target to work toward empowers a person. The dreams list functions as the inspiring target, which makes it incredibly powerful.

Argument 2: Dreaming Is Fun

When someone buys a lottery ticket, there's a moment of "What if I win?" Most people think, "What would I do with the winnings?" Even though you know there's a low chance that you're going to win, in that moment, there's this weird dream phase that goes something like, "I would buy a new X. I could afford a better Y. Wow!" Call it a lottery ticket high. A "What If" buzz.

It's easy to experience a similar trancey buzz when you have a great idea. It happens after the idea is conceived, but before it's realized. The same is true when you plan a great vacation. It happens after tickets are booked, but before the ride to the airport departures lounge. The in-between place is exciting. It is full of anticipation—a space of wonder, excitement, and delightful speculation of what's to come.

What if we had extended periods of the What If buzz? Let's just say you had at least two of those buzzes each year. That'd probably be a pretty good year. What if you had four? Or six? Or even more? What if your entire year was stacked with those moments of elated anticipation? Rinse and repeat. An endless possibilities shampoo. Would you get more out of your day? Would you be more efficient with your time at work so you could be done with work? Would you be healthier in your choices? A young man who works on our team has taken this concept and run with it. Alex Funk was introduced to this concept in 2019. In 2020 he completed thirty-six dreams. Many of these are small, but he always has something in his calendar that he is moving toward.

These are questions to ask retreat attendees. They help people immediately lock into the value of the Stage 1 dreamstorming sessions. The group must be given permission to linger in the What If space. Set their rational mind aside. It's not needed now, nor is it useful while dreamstorming.

Dreaming brings a quality of fun to life. It makes people feel good. And that's not only great for them, it's great for the people around them because the positivity it breeds is infectious.

When even one person on a team is in a positive mood they raise the good-vibe quotient for the rest. There's a scientific term for this phenomenon: positive contagion. One particular study of fifty-six self-managed teams determined that "leader positive moods positively predicted group coordination via increasing positive group affective tone."[11] In other words, positive contagions (moods) from one person leading the charge on feeling good led to improved team performance.

Dream thinking is enjoyable. It raises the levels of joy, fun, and playfulness for the entire team.

Few people ever get to spend a day thinking about their future. Even fewer are told to do it at work. (Although my aim with this book is to change that.) That's what a dreamstorming session is for.

Getting participants to embrace being playful, though, can be tougher than it might appear. People default to rational thinking. And often at work or with their coworkers, practical is not only their default state, but a foundation they cling to. It's safe. So once you have the agreement of the room, you want to show them there is massive value to dreams. To do this, use leverage.

Step 2:
Use Leverage

In Chapter 2, we talked about how dream thinking is natural when we're kids and how it usually gets conditioned out of us as we age. People learn to be rational.

There's value to being practical, but it can also hold people back. Finding a balance is ideal so you can toggle between imagination, which is controlled by the right brain, and logic, which is the domain of the left brain.

Using a tactic called *leverage,* I use undisputed facts to get people to appreciate the value of dream thinking. Leverage is about acknowledging a key pain point the person has and making a case for why you have the solution.

Leverage Argument #1:
Dreams Increase Positive Thoughts
and Feelings

Mental health is at its worst in trackable history. I'm writing this during the pandemic when people are struggling the most. Having a purpose isn't just nice, it's critical for sustaining well-being during tough times. People are not good at harvesting hope from external sources, like the media or through the pleasure of a shopping spree, or from reading about the economy. Dreams give hope, and hope gives people strength in difficult times. Dreams give people an internal source of motivation separate from what they get from society and their environment.

Research conducted in November of 2020, nine months into the pandemic, by Katelyn N.G. Young found that participants who had a greater sense of hope also rated higher on mental and physical health.[12] "A greater sense of hope was associated with: better physical health and health behavior outcomes on some indicators (e.g., reduced risk of all cause-mortality, fewer number of chronic conditions, lower risk of cancer, and fewer sleep problems), and higher psychological well-being (e.g., increased positive affect, life satisfaction, and purpose in life), lower psychological distress, and better social well-being."

Dreams give people hope. And hope is more important than most people think it is.

When you share this with a group, it's a statement that gets nods from across the room. As I speak, it is obvious their wheels are turning. People start engaging in their own journey and making sense of what I'm saying. So I use several leverage tactics at this point. Different people are compelled by different ideas so always use more than one type of leverage to get the group where you need them to be.

Leverage Argument #2:
Being a Dreamer Makes You a Highly
Prized Asset at Work

Dream thinkers are assets in the workplace. Innovators are needed today in business more than ever before. Bringing this argument helps career-driven teammates see how taking dreams seriously will make them a highly prized commodity at work.

In April 2020, an article published by *Harvard Business Review* titled "We Need Imagination Now More Than Ever" reported, "Pandemics, wars, and other social crises often create new attitudes, needs, and behaviors, which need to be managed... imagination—the capacity to create, evolve, and exploit mental models of things or situations that don't yet exist—is the crucial factor in seizing and creating new opportunities, and finding new paths to growth."

Never underestimate the importance of daydreaming, critical thinking, and learning. These are the building blocks of innovation.

"'Creativity is the rearrangement of existing knowledge into new, useful combinations,' said Jorgen Vig Knudstorp, Chairman of the Lego Brand Group. 'Just like playing with LegoBricks, this can lead you to valuable innovations—like the Google search engine or the Airbnb business model.'"[13]

As bestselling author and marketing expert Seth Godin writes in his book *Linchpin*, "The linchpins among us are not the ones born with a magical talent. No, they are people who have decided that a new kind of work is important, and trained themselves to do it."[14]

To be seen as truly dynamic, highly skilled, and an asset on any team, dream. Checking dream lists in our personal lives correlates to higher performance at work. Because, again, we don't have a work life and a personal life, we have one life.

Leverage Argument #3: Dreams Are Kind of Why We're Here, Right?

Aren't we here to live our dream lives? Doesn't it make sense to set targets and always have them in place to be building a life that's fulfilling? Intentionally interrupting busy lives to reflect on where we are going is an important practice. Yet so many people don't carve out the time to do the work.

When I introduce this idea, many people see it as a wake-up call. They realize it is their responsibility to stay inspired and only engage in the activities that light them up.

You will need to adapt this argument to the room demographics. For instance, for a group of Gen Xers, I might ask them to personalize it by asking when was the last time they took a big family vacation or engaged in a hobby they really love. I might even suggest that they pick up the phone to call their brother who lives in Europe.

It's easy to go on autopilot mode in life. And so, the dreams are kind of why we're here, right? It's a simple way to have people get serious and reflect about dreams they've put on hold.

Leverage Argument #4:
Who Are You for the People
Around You?

Most evolved parents tell their kids they can become or have anything they want. They encourage their children to live passionately and pursue happiness over material goods.

Have a group reflect on the example they are setting for their kids by the way they live their lives. Ask them to pause and reflect: are we practicing what we preach?

Most people agree that it's important to be an example for the next generation, to do our part to leave the world a better place. So beyond being an example for kids, and because some people don't have kids, another question to ask is: how do we inspire the people around us?

Social psychology studies demonstrate that an individual's behavior, temperament, and actions are tied to the people who are three degrees or less of separation from them. What that means is, if your partner starts eating healthier, it's likely you will too. They are one degree of separation from you. If your mother-in-law, who lives six hours away, gets a gym membership and starts focusing on her health, it's likely she'll impact your spouse.

And, your mother-in-law's cousin, who Zooms with her regularly from Germany, might have started it all. She influenced her, and your partner, and now you. Wild, isn't it?

How are you influencing the people in your social sphere?

Our social networks impact our lives. Research from Harvard University sociologist Nicholas Christakis and University of California San Diego political scientist James Fowler found that behaviors, "spread among people up to three degrees of separation."[15] So dreamers are more likely to encourage their friends, family, and neighbors to dream too.

Leverage Argument #5:
Dream Lists Are Not Bucket Lists

It's important to make the distinction that the work at the retreat is not to build a list of dreams a person may or may not ever get to. I usually say, "This isn't a list of things that you're never going to do. It's not a bucket list. Or something you are going to work to complete by the time you are eighty." Many people can think of someone they know who retired and, shortly after, passed away. We don't know how long we have with this life. We shouldn't wait to live it until we are in our later years.

Encourage them to let their imagination run wild and create an exhaustive list of hundreds of dreams during this first stage.

Later, in Stage 3—Dream Planning, they'll zero in on dreams they want to make happen now and create action plans.

For dreamstorming to be effective, your attendees will need to dump their rational thinking. Budget doesn't matter. Time doesn't matter. The occupation that they have right now with the company doesn't matter. These factors aren't important for this phase.

Step 3:
Set Expectations

Finally, set expectations on behavior. There are three qualities that participants can embrace to get the most out of what they're doing. Like anything in life, effort matches results. I find the following phrase is helpful to include in the presentation:

"Be engaged. Be open-minded. Be willing to open up a bit more than usual."

Challenge your team to embrace these three qualities for the duration of the dreamstorming session:

- Engagement

- Abundance Mindset

- Vulnerability

Show them what each one looks like in practice because people might have their own ideas.

Engagement

Ask your team to ignore current demands for their time and to do their best to be fully present. They might have reports that didn't get done sitting on their desks in the office. Or emails they haven't answered. Maybe they are still thinking about the fight they had with their significant other the night before.

Whatever it is, invite the team to be here now. Ask them to set their phone to do not disturb mode. Give them time to wrap up any items that may be mentally drawing their attention away.

Abundance Mindset

Encourage attendees to do their best to think with no practical constraints. It's common that people will get inspired by an idea then switch back to rational thinking. They might think they have limited time off, or they can't afford it, or they are too old to achieve it.

Brainstorming effectively is a no-constraints process. Same with dreamstorming. To encourage abundance thinking I might use this example: "Think of yourself in peak health right now. What could you do?" That's the abundance mindset sweet spot. Just go for it. Put it on the list.

That's the idea. I also will take people through the exercise of examples rather quickly and repeat numerous times, "If it sounds cool, jot it down."

Vulnerability

Tell the room that later you will invite people to share, but also tell them it will be an invitation and is not mandatory. They get serious value from sharing, but ultimately, they choose what they are comfortable telling the group.

During Stage 1—Dreamstorming, they just need to be honest with themselves. Remind them that the process is private. No one is watching or judging what they write on their list.

Remind them they don't have to confront or compare their dreams with those of others in the room. Some people will suppress what they truly want because they're afraid of judgment or comparison. Encourage them to write freeform and let the ideas flow. Later, when sharing happens, they don't have to share any dreams they aren't comfortable sharing.

But being vulnerable starts with being straight with themselves. That is when they will get the most out of the work. I'll also share some weird examples of dreams to open up the group.

Once you set expectations and there is agreement in the room, dive in. Now you can begin the work of Stage 1—Dreamstorming.

THE DREAMSTORMING PROCESS

The intention of dreamstorming is to give people time to create a large list of ideas that inspires them in all the key areas of their life. At this point, the idea is to think abundantly. Deliberating on what gets put on the list or not should be limited. They will revise the list later.

Some people might feel confused, stressed, or nervous around doing it right.

So it's useful to remind them that this is a living document that they can add to or change later. This is like hitting a "chill out" button for some people in the room.

Personally, I constantly add and subtract from my list. I have a section in my notes app on my phone for dreams. When I'm out and about in life I get ideas. I commonly stop, get inspired, and think: ooh, that's going on the list. Then, I pull my dreams list out and add it immediately.

My master dreams list lives on my laptop, but I keep a working list on my phone so I can remember my inspirational bursts and add them to my laptop later.

Freeform Writing Is Most Effective

Making an exhaustive list of dreams can at first seem daunting. Or sometimes people have ideas and then start reeling themselves back in. Remember, overly practical thinking is not useful.

The best approach is to scribble down whatever comes to mind first and go fast. Freeform writing is the way to do it.

Writing freeform, also known as automatic writing, helps people activate their creative, right-brain thinking versus using their rational mind. Modern psychodynamic theories of personality propose that attitudes, motives, and memories that are incompatible with a person's conscious awareness aren't always expressed. Deeper ideas may be revealed by using the process of freeform writing. It can help people tune into subconscious thoughts and deep desire.

The bottom line is: being practical cuts off the flow of ideas.

Now, when brainstorming, the first ideas aren't always the best. But that's okay too. This brings me to my next point, to remind the team that dreams are iterative.

Like All Great Ideas, Dreams Are Iterative

In the book *Originals: How Non-Conformists Move the World*, author Adam Grant explains how innovators aren't people who always have great ideas. Instead, they are people who generate a massive abundance of ideas. Grant writes about how one of Maya Angelou's most famous poems was written 165 times. He also discusses how Thomas Edison tried 1,000 unsuccessful times before inventing a light bulb that worked. Grant explains, "Creativity is allowing yourself to make mistakes. Art is knowing which ones to keep."

The more dreams written down on a list, the more massive the menu to choose from later. The creation of a dreams list should begin as a sloppy brain dump of ideas. A person should then pare it down and refine from there.

The Nine-Category Rollout

Since dream thinking requires an easing in for some people, I've developed a list of nine categories that I roll out during the dreamstorming session. Here's the flow:

1. Travel

2. Adventure

3. Material

4. Financial/Career

5. Family/Relationships

6. Health

7. Creativity/Skills

8. Faith/Spirituality

9. Legacy

I typically start with travel because it is usually the largest category and the easiest to brainstorm. It's usually simple for someone to look at a world map and say, "Yeah, that'd be a cool place to go."

I always make a point to emphasize again how critical it is not to be restrictive. I'll say, "If you hear something today and you think, 'I never thought about that, but that'd be cool,' put it on the list and explore it later."

The American Express monthly magazine has inspired many of my dream places. When I flip through the pages I commonly see glossy photos of exotic locales I've never heard of before like Arashiyama Bamboo Forest in Japan, or the Forest of Knives in Madagascar, which are now on my list.

There are 196 countries in the world (recognized by the US), each with hundreds of cities, towns, and interesting sites to visit.

Travel is a category your participants can spend a lot of time on. That is another reason to put it first. Start regionally, expand nationally, then consider destinations all over the world. This is the simplest way for people to think about it.

Encourage the team to be open to whatever comes up. "If Italy pops in your head as I'm talking about pizza in New York City, throw it on there," I'll say. In other words, nobody is checking anyone's assignment here. The idea is to just go for it. That is the spirit the room should embrace.

Travel is easy to start with because it's a natural category people dream often about. The progression of categories is by design. It starts light with travel and adventure, then moves to areas people focus on often and take more seriously like career and finances, and relationships and health. The more abstract or serious topics come near the end. They are spirituality and legacy. Those topics require deeper introspection.

The flow is intentional to help ease people into the process. It also embraces the light and fun nature of the process first and progresses to the more serious personal topics as people get used to flexing their dreamstorming muscle.

It's always smart to tweak the category rollout based on the group that's in the room. For instance, if you're doing this with a group of athletes you might move the health goals up toward the beginning.

Or if you're leading a church group, faith might be a great second or third category because it's a top priority for that group.

At this point in your dreamstorming session you can expect the room to be quietly buzzing. Watch people's eyes.

They will give away their bursts of excitement but also show their engagement in their list. The only person speaking should be the leader, however small side chatter happens and can be a good sign. Their job is to help the group think creatively, so at each phase ideas are planted, images are shown, and personal stories are pivotal for triggering dream thinking. I call them thought joggers.

Use Thought Joggers

A thought jogger stimulates dream thinking by presenting lots of ideas by demonstrating dreams of others. Show dreams that you or people you know have accomplished. Share stories. Post pictures. Videos are also great.

Thought joggers help people expand their lists using ideas that they may not have considered on their own. What's easier? Making a list of places you want to travel to by looking at a map of the world or seeing pictures of places you have never been to. If I show a photo of my trip to Croatia, you might think, *Wow, Croatia is stunning!* And then it goes on your list.

Or what if I told you a story of a friend of mine who has traveled to seventy-nine countries and I mention Moldova. Maybe you wouldn't consider that on your own but add it after you hear how cool it is. (And here I'm hinting at the value of dream sharing, but we'll get to that in the next chapter.)

Thought joggers are especially useful for analytical people. They help people get inspired by giving them examples to consider and build on. Always include examples of small and big dreams, and use weird examples too.

Why Weird Works

Dreams don't need to be all big ideas. Some dreams are small, like flossing for thirty days straight. As I mentioned earlier, Robert, a member of my personal team, put this down and then celebrated accomplishing it during one for the first months of the COVID-19 lockdown. What a way to spend your time in isolation, ha!

And since the way people think is as unique as their DNA, it makes sense that some dreams are weird. Encourage weird ideas by making them less weird with examples.

Zorbing is one example of a weird dream I achieved. I did it with coworkers as a fun reward day for thirty people who reached a top sales quota that year. Every chance I get, I'll share details from that day. The group always finds them hilarious too.

Imagine adults wearing giant inflatable bubble ball suits. That is what zorbing is. You can battle in them or play games. In these Zorbing Bubbles, only your legs are exposed beneath the knee, so they allow you to run around and ricochet off other people. So you're running around, playing kids' games like red rover, red rover. We also played full contact soccer. It was hilarious because nobody was even looking at the ball. Everybody was instead trying to knock each other down. Even people who are in great shape can only zorb for five minutes max before they need a break. I don't know what was more fun, participating or just watching other people run around in them. Either way, it was a big win!

Sharing weird examples of dreams allows people to be creative and more authentic. It helps them access odd or unusual ideas without self-censure.

THE MIRACLE
OF WONDER AT WORK

During the process of writing this book, my office in Minneapolis was ranked No. 1 in the company, and my division was No. 3. It was a dream my team created. And months away from our end-of-year target I was blown away by how my team had developed their capacity to dream. They had become big dreamers. In a group text, I watched people share the "anything's possible" chatter and a flow of enthusiastic innovative ideas on how we could achieve more. I reveled in the fact that my team was almost more excited than me, the division leader.

People who dreamstorm get used to an "anything's possible" mindset. Then, the excitement of reaching an outcome is enough to propel them forward to take massive action and increase the odds of achieving results. That's why sharing dreams is another structure we'll discuss.

Once people go through the dreamstorming process, they learn the value of thinking about categories of life from multiple angles. This same process can be brought to work to innovate on systems, products, or services. It happens naturally the more a person develops their dreamstorming ability.

Up next is Stage 2—Dream Sharing & Stealing. It brings dreams immediately into reality, helps them happen faster, and expands ideas. It's the second critical phase of dream-planning success.

CHAPTER 5

DREAM SHARING AND STEALING

IN 2020, A HAPPINESS experiment shared on YouTube went viral.[16] A teacher had each of his students write their name on an inflated balloon he gave them. The balloons were then randomly tossed into a hallway at school.

He then mixed up the balloons and said to his class, "You each have five minutes to find your balloon." None of the students was successful. When the five minutes was up, each kid stood in the hall, colored balloons around their feet, staring blankly at each other. Everyone was empty-handed.

"Now, pick up the balloon closest to you, find the person whose name it has on it, and give it to them as fast as possible," the teacher then said. Within two minutes each child had the balloon with their name on it.

The teacher designed this experiment to teach a critical life lesson: Each balloon represents a person's happiness. When a person is focused on their own happiness it's more difficult to find than when it's their job to help someone else find happiness.

It's no surprise this sweet video went viral. When people turn their focus outward, making it their responsibility to ensure the happiness of another, the person they are focused on gets what they want faster. In return, the happiness maker gets taken care of too. They are more likely to get support from the happiness receiver as well.

You've likely experienced this form of reciprocal generosity in a relationship before, maybe a romantic one. It tends to happen when two people fall in love. Early on in a relationship, most people are doing everything to woo and impress the lover they want to make theirs.

Each party goes all-in on causing their partner's happiness. Person A focuses on the fulfillment of Person B, and the opposite is also true. Now, neither person has to stress out or get too caught up in themselves. Not only that, it's so much easier and more fun to focus on the happiness of someone else, right? This is one key reason why dream sharing is such a special and critical part of the Dreams Retreat.

Personal dreams aside, the "I've got your back, you've got mine" reciprocal dynamic is the foundation of the best business teams too. It is equally valuable at work. When people are bonded by a mission and care as much about their colleagues' success as their own, they achieve remarkable outcomes faster.

This is one of the serious benefits available from a Stage 2—Dream Sharing session. Colleagues connect there and then carry dream conversations into work, which leads to stronger bonds and better performance on work projects too.

For companies across the globe, our biggest challenge is keeping up with the rate of change itself. During crisis situations like a global pandemic, a strong team is what made or broke a business. Top leaders in business know that teams where people are committed to each other's greatness perform better. In his book *Beyond Entrepreneurship 2.0*, Jim Collins explains that a culture where people depend on each other always beats a culture driven by financial incentives, especially today in a disrupted business landscape.[17]

Keith Ferrazzi, executive coach and Founder of Ferrazzi Greenlight, a Los Angeles-based business research and consulting firm, wrote the bestselling book *Leading Without Authority*.[18] His term for this type of value exchange in relationships is co-elevation. It means to "go higher together." The idea is, I commit to your greatness and you commit to mine. It's easier to help someone win and, at the same time, reduce the effort needed to succeed yourself.

To truly support another person, and to establish a relationship where people have each other's back, each person must invite the other person into their world. They must be willing to share what's important to them. And that's not always easy. A person must cross a vulnerability threshold to do this. Dream sharing gets people to do this in a way that's fun, light, and easy.

In fact, it really is fun. But more than that, there are five key reasons why it is an essential part of the Dreams Retreat process:

1. Sharing is a bridge that helps ideas become realized.

2. Sharing deepens bonds.

3. Sharing speeds results.

4. Sharing makes dreams easier to achieve.

5. Sharing expands ideas.

This chapter explores why dream sharing is at the center of Phase Two. But first let me provide the context for sharing.

The act of sharing itself is more than a vehicle of communication where an idea or information is transmitted from one person to the next. It's a power tool that connects two or more people and turns them into a co-creative community where collaboration happens and personal goals and team outcomes are achieved faster.

Dream sharing is not only a critical part of the process for people reaching their dreams, it is also a way to build a creative and collaborative work culture.

SHARING IS A BRIDGE THAT HELPS IDEAS BECOME REALIZED

T o build a true dream culture, people must take action and not just write lists.

Pursuing and achieving dreams is the entire reason for this work, so it would make sense to have structures to carry through on dreams beyond the initial brainstorming work. The first very basic step to making any idea or dream a reality is to speak it out loud so other people can hear it.

Dream sharing is the first time a person declares publicly what they want, which is often the very first step to making it real. Sharing is a bridge that allows any concept to go from the land of thought to a tangible reality.

An idea has little value unless it is acted upon. A notepad filled with ideas, or a document on Google Drive, serves no purpose unless it's put into action. Dreams often remain dreams simply because people don't share them—usually because there's typically no structured time to do it.

Sometimes people are afraid of their bold ideas. If they want to write a book or do more public speaking or lose a significant amount of weight, there needs to be a moment of reckoning, where the idea moves from concept to reality. That happens when the idea is shared and then acted upon.

If a person is willing to be honest and vulnerable, they just might be brave enough to speak what they authentically want in front of other people. Then once it's out there, they can't deny it anymore. It becomes real.

While writing dreams down is a useful frame, vocalizing them provides the cement that makes them solid. It reinforces the idea back to the speaker because they've put it out there. Public accountability helps here too.

Most people are hardwired to not want to look bad in front of their family, friends, and peers. This is called impression management, and it's done to enhance self-esteem and gain social reward/prominence.[19] Want to turn a dream into reality? Tell someone.

When you do, you'll find your idea might expand from there with their support and encouragement. Speaking any dream into existence is somewhat of a magical moment. We can't help but accept it ourselves. It becomes a little more possible the moment it is spoken. And, if it still seems hard to achieve, at least we've confronted it.

I get to see this happen firsthand when I facilitate Dreams Retreats for other organizations. Watching people get inspired when their teammates share their dreams is powerful. Oftentimes, they've been working together for years and discover new dimensions to one another.

It happened recently when I was facilitating with NGNG (No Guts, No Glory) Enterprises. Their team works remotely so their interactions are all on Zoom. During the dream-sharing session I was bouncing around to various breakout rooms and was astounded by the inspiring shares and deeper connections that took place.

"I really want to cage dive with sharks," one woman shared with her colleagues. Then the next woman in the same room read some dreams on her list. "I've always wanted to live off the land," she said.

These aren't usual work conversations. When colleagues have extra time on a Zoom they might ask, "Hey, how's the family?" but very rarely do they dive deep enough on personal dreams to really understand the unique ideas and true brilliance of each other. It's amazing to hear these types of shares and see how people learn and hold each other accountable.

You simply can't hold a person to account if they don't share their dream, because it remains a secret in a dark corner of their head. You can't contribute to it either to help them make it a reality.

Sharing Makes Dreams
Possible Faster

At our 2020 Dreams Retreat, Rachel wrote on her dreams list: "Get more into my faith." She later came to me with a request: "Hey, Dane, can I ask the team if there is anyone else who would like to be in a Bible study group? I'd like to start one."

I told her to pitch the idea, as long as the study group would be run outside of work time. That year, Rachel wasn't the only one who wanted to develop their faith. Her request to launch a group prompted several of her colleagues to join in. The group still runs today, helping its members strengthen their faith. It's given them all a spiritual group to turn to for support, which certainly is a helpful resilience structure that also supports great performance at work.

When dreams are shared, teams can build smaller communities to accomplish dreams together. By putting it out there, connections organically form. And that doesn't happen until people speak what they want out loud.

It's also common to see new alliances form. Dreams get accomplished faster when colleagues realize they have resources to help each other out. This type of scenario is common, Steve stands up and addresses the group saying: "I wrote on my list that I'd like to learn more about investing in real estate and buying a property to create rental income."

Later, when the session wraps, I see Melanie chatting with him. She tells him that her cousin invests in real estate and offers to connect them. A few months later, Steve has his first investment property, which would have taken him a year or more to figure out had he not attended the Dreams Retreat.

When people share dreams with each other they buy into what the other person wants to achieve, and often, even more than their own dreams. I think it feels as good, if not better, to help somebody else accomplish their dream as it does when you work on your own dreams, though the perfect combination is both. There is nothing better than accomplishing your own dreams and helping other people achieve theirs.

Sharing Deepens Bonds

When people share their dreams, other people get to know them better. It moves relationships past the surface level and deepens them. It is beautiful to see people connect in new ways, to discover each other's awesomeness, and to hear about their families, their backgrounds, and their lives outside of work. Watching people help each other is equally gratifying.

New friendships form. People make deeper connections. Partners sync up. All this speeds up the rate of achieving dreams together. There are times where they form groups and accomplish dreams as a community too. Just take Rachel's Bible study group. The work environment is rarely a place where people share their spirituality, let alone help each other deepen it. But Rachel achieved that simply by sharing a dream she wrote down on a sheet of paper.

A bonded team is a byproduct that comes naturally from Stage 2—Dream Sharing & Stealing, and that certainly increases retention.[20]

Employees with friends at work are more likely to love their company and stay longer. Globoforce led a study for *Workforce Magazine* that surveyed 716 full-time US employees. Of those with six to twenty-five friends at work, almost two-thirds reported loving their company and 70 percent said they would reject a job offer elsewhere.

Work is also more enjoyable with friends. A bonded culture is fun to work in. It's nice to feel at home at work, more like a family than a group of people connected by their paycheck who show up in business attire, sit at computers, and only talk in between PowerPoint presentations.

Sharing Expands Ideas

Did it ever occur to you that something wasn't a dream of yours until you learned it was possible? In other words, there was a point in your life that you didn't even know what a marathon was before it became a goal you wanted to achieve? People run 26.2 miles all at once? Really? It came from a distance that the ancient Greeks ran? Another obvious reason why dream sharing is a critical component to the process.

I experienced this when I shifted from making my own dream lists to sharing them with my wife. Brookelynn started talking about her dreams too. Together we started knocking out dreams, which, as you'll recall, led to our annual tradition of an end-of-the-year dream-planning date. Doing this also strengthens our marriage.

The beauty of sharing with Brookelynn taught me early on how dreams expand and become much better when they're shared. Every person looks at life through their own lens, which is based on their own upbringing and individual experiences. Take someone who grew up on a rural farm with little access to the internet. They might have no idea about traveling to Vietnam.

For a generation it was the location of an unpopular war. Until somebody exposes them to the idea that a modern reunified Vietnam is now a thriving country with great food and culture and an exotic destination for travelers, they might never consider it. Sharing with others is how new dreams are generated, expanded on, and made more possible.

It's spectacular when a person's mind opens up to new opportunities they never conceived. Or when another person shares a small idea that expands so much that it moves into the realm of possibility.

Sharing inspires others. And when you hear someone share a good dream, **it's time to steal it.**

Dream Stealing

During dream sharing I encourage everyone to dream steal. I remind them that when they share their dreams they will inevitably cause someone else to light up. Remember, dream sharing is a gift you give to others because it often causes inspiration. That is why I highly encourage dream stealing. The idea is, when you hear a dream share that you like, write it down.

Getting a custom-made suit was a dream idea I stole early on. I did that in Thailand and it was an experience I'll never forget.

It was such a cool experience that I've even gifted a similar experience to people at work. Unfortunately for them it wasn't in Thailand, but it was still a great experience for them to have someone come and help them customize their own suit.

I steal a lot of travel dreams. Browsing through social media, I like to cherry pick travel ideas from people's posts. One travel destination on my list that I found using this technique is Dubrovnik, Croatia. Look it up. It is a stunning city that fronts the sparkling Adriatic Sea, surrounded by medieval century walls and filled with cobblestone streets lined with world-class restaurants. Feel free to steal it from me. Put it on your list if you're so inspired.

LEADING THE DREAM– SHARING PROCESS

Most people find this stage fun and interactive. You'll recall that in Stage 1—Dreamstorming the room is typically quiet. Everyone is listening to the speaker and engrossed in their own list-building process.

But in Stage 2—Dream Sharing & Stealing, the energy dynamic of the room shifts, moving from internal contemplation into the community in the room. It's playful because sharing ideas is generally fun. Unlike at work, no one is being forced to innovate on a particular solution. This type of collaboration is a relaxed, easy, and joyful experience.

Before you begin the dream-sharing process, give participants a break, I find that at least two hours should be given, though it could be an entire afternoon. They've all just been heads down deeply thinking. For some people the ideas are new, maybe even scary. The process to come up with dreams can be mentally taxing and can be confrontational for some. But for most, it's an exciting process. A break is welcome and often necessary for people to pause and decompress. Give people time with no agenda, to hang out, eat food, play games, do whatever.

At our events we will usually encourage people to grab some food and spend time together outdoors. You'll find that much of the conversation that's happening is about the exercise they just went through.

Then bring the group back for dream sharing. They just got done socializing, so it's not hard for them to shift into a light and fun mode for the next part of the event.

Split the Team into Small Groups

During this second phase of the dream-planning process, split the group into smaller subgroups. I find that groups of eight or less work great. Each member will be asked to take turns sharing dreams from each of the categories. I instruct them to spend a few minutes picking the dreams they'd like to share. We ask them to share five from the travel, adventure, material, financial/career, family/relationship, health, and creativity categories, and three from faith/spirituality and legacy.

We encourage them to share whatever they'd like; they can choose ones they are most excited about, ones they think are the most unique, or the most normal. It is time for people to focus on their peers, and each participant takes a turn to share in the smaller group.

Small groups keep the mood intimate. It's also nice to keep departments together at first. It's valuable when Rob's team or Janet's team knows about each person's dreams. When they see their colleagues on a day-to-day basis they can hold each other accountable if applicable.

There can be a benefit to mixing teams too. A company that wants colleagues from different teams to build relationships may find cross-functional groups useful. You could put sales with accounting or operations with procurement teams. Do whatever makes the most sense for your company's dynamic.

Then, once the teams are formed, we give a few instructions and off they go. We encourage them to go round robin and have everyone share their travel category before moving on to the next category. One of the reasons that we do this is to build larger lists.

Again, expectation setting is key here. Reminders are great. "All right. So what's most important now is engagement. Please put your phones away and get present, and embrace an abundance mindset," I'll say.

Remind them to reserve judgment. It sometimes takes vulnerability to share a dream you're passionate about. Everyone should feel free in this room to do that.

If someone says, "I'd love to go to the moon," you might think that is not possible. But critiquing ideas is not the job at hand. Instead, listen and receive. When possible, share uplifting supporting examples. Recently, I had the opportunity to hear former NASA Astronaut Leroy Chiao speak at a "Jam Session" put on by the Prouty Project, and he mentioned that going to outer space was always a **dream** of his as a child. He just never gave up on it.

During this phase there is a lot of chatter and that's a good thing.

I always encourage the group to allow the sharer to have the floor, but I'm always intentional not to try to squelch a group's dynamic. You'll notice that many groups will be laughing and having a great time. That's great. Let people have fun.

But also, explain that they should not offer advice. Coach participants to simply embrace what is shared. People might share ideas they've never shared with work people before. Set the stage beforehand to make them feel comfortable. Understand that it's natural for people to say "my friend did that a few years ago..." These types of statements are a great way for people to connect and this should be encouraged by the facilitator.

BEYOND THE RETREAT

Within my organization, sharing beyond the retreat is optional. They know the company is fully invested in supporting everyone to live their dreams and inspire others to do the same. But they also know that it's on them to take initiative, to share, to take the actions to make their dreams happen.

That said, I never end a Stage 2—Dream Sharing & Stealing without inviting people to continue to share at work after the Dreams Retreat. "I would love for you to share your dreams list with me, the whole thing, a portion of it, whatever you feel comfortable with," I'll say. "If it were up to me, I'd love to see 100 percent of your dreams!"

This invitation lines up with our dreams culture. It also helps the company use dreams as an incentive. Corporate dollars put to dreams is what you'll learn about in Chapter 7.

CHAPTER 6

DREAM PLANNING

MINNESOTA WINTERS ARE HARSH. Snow and ice is regular and the cold can be disheartening. Yet, it was under these subzero conditions that I launched a dream one January day a few years back. The objective: run a marathon in June.

But to do that required some serious forethought and planning. Training had to start months before the race. And the action I needed to take that first day required me to crawl from the warm cocoon of my bed, shiver, shiver again, then, with envy, look at my fiancée still swaddled and snoozing. Still, my commitment to fulfill the dream was stronger than my desire for comfort. So I pulled on my Nike running gear that made me look way faster and more of a runner than I actually was. Moments later I scooted out the door and ran into the frigid air, drawing in fine ice crystals with each labored breath.

I didn't love my morning runs at first. They weren't pretty. But I got them done anyway. And it wasn't long before the icy pacing through the crisp mornings became a routine I enjoyed.

After six weeks of training, the burning lungs and the aching legs became insignificant as my body adjusted to the conditions and the exertion. The discomfort faded and I felt as if I never wanted to live without this time. It was precious. The stillness of the world and the sky still dark and slowly shifting from navy to a sunlit soft blue was wonderful to witness. I always ran listening to an audiobook or podcast on business or leadership, which made it an almost spiritual practice.

By month three I reflected how this was not the Dane I'd known for years. He was definitely not a runner. I would never have predicted it. It was a dream I put in action that pulled me, in no time, toward a new version of me, Dane the marathon runner.

"I'm going to run a marathon this year," I had said to Brookelynn heading into that year. She was sitting across from me at our dining room table on New Year's Eve. We were having our second annual dream-planning date and what had come up for me were a lot of dreams about being in better shape. Honestly, it had not been a big focus for me until that moment. But I was in my upper twenties now and I didn't have the energy or ability to consume gratuitous calories with no waistline penalty, as I had in my early years. I had gained a bit of weight and needed a structure that would keep me consistently in the gym.

"Book it," she said excitedly. I googled a few options, found a local marathon six months out—a few clicks and taps on the keyboard and it was done. There was a June race in my home city, so I paid my registration fee right there. Boom, it was done. Now, I was running a race.

Every morning I got up around 5:00 a.m., providing my routine and structure to get in shape and to log the hundreds of miles of training needed to be able to complete the 26.2 miles of a marathon race.

On June 1, 2014, I woke up super early to prepare for race day and get to the starting line. To my disappointment, it was storming pretty badly. I packed my stuff up and got out to the starting line only to have the entire race canceled due to inclement weather.

It was a false start but I was surprisingly cool with it. I learned that the anticipation and pursuing of a dream matters more than actually accomplishing that dream. I had four to five months of extremely consistent workouts and was in great shape.

I signed up for the same race the following year and completed that as my first marathon.

After months of training and grinding through 26.2 miles of the race, crossing a marathon finish line was surreal.

The crowd that lines the route to cheer you on is the best part. You reach the part where every muscle in your body is yelling at you to stop, but the cheers from the people keep you going, especially in the last few miles. At about the twenty-mile mark you hit what is called "The Wall." It is the point when a runner's glycogen, a sugar that converts to energy, is depleted. If you have ever seen a distance runner wobble on their legs, that's the end product of the wall. Some runners slow to a staggering walk. Others collapse. Some run-walk through the final miles powered by a fierce will to finish.

I saw my wife along the way five to six times that day. Stepping across that finish line was an amazing feeling that I'm so grateful to have. It was pure nirvana. It all seemed to happen in slow motion, a blur, and strangely, dream-like. When I crossed over that divine line it was all worth it.

The $150 marathon entry fee was a good investment. The payment is a motivator that helps you hold yourself to account against what you promised. Weirdly, that $150 also paid back other dividends. I lost twenty pounds that spring and got into the best shape that I had been in in years. It shouldn't need to be like that truly, but that's the way that most people's brains work. If we cement a future structure with something tangible like an entry fee, or an air ticket, it creates a mental anchor that massively increases the likelihood of executing and fulfilling a plan. And in my case, realizing a dream.

Success in making my dreams a reality didn't always happen. As you'll recall, after hearing Matthew Kelly speak, I wrote my first dreams list in a Word document. I dutifully titled it Dane's Dream List then saved it on my computer. And then I quickly forgot about it.

There was a major flaw in my system. I had no process to put my dreams into action. Writing the list made me focus more on what I wanted to achieve, but I still was not methodical about the follow-through. This is the step most people trip on when it comes to fulfilling dreams, or any goal in life, for that matter.

Still, the abandoned list had produced some results. I had written down: "Run a million-dollar office." I accomplished that two years later. A big dream fulfilled, for sure, demonstrating that just the act of writing a dream down can increase the chance of fulfilling it. That fact is backed by neuroscience.

That list also contained many dreams that remained unfulfilled, because I didn't have an action plan. My process was broken.

Again, I thought of Tony Robbins, who espouses: "Take action in a peak state." If you take action right away when you are all lit up about some wild idea, the odds of making it happen increase massively. Using the momentum of a positive emotional state will carry you through, and often, help overcome the nerves that set in once a commitment is made.

Writing your dreams is an important step that you learned in Chapter 4. Putting them out there and sharing with people around you is a critical step that creates a simple accountability system. In his book *Triggers*, Marshall Goldsmith talks about the value of having an accountability check-in person.[21] It's critical.

But that's not enough. The people that you share your dreams with will rarely follow up with you. They're all dealing with their own stuff. They have their own life, goals, and dreams to worry about. So you can't expect them to check in every week and ask you how those 5 a.m. winter training runs are going for you.

You have to put dreams into action immediately using a schedule.

It makes them concrete and it's harder to forget about them when—DING—Google Calendar pops open and says: Buy blister Band-Aids for training runs on weekends. Creating an action plan isn't just useful, there's science that backs up why it makes sense.

THE SCIENCE OF
AN IMPLEMENTATION PLAN

C hange can equal growth if it's intentional. So when a person immediately changes their calendar, it increases their chances of taking new steps to grow. The value of increasing your chances of changing is immeasurable if you consider how easy it is to fall back into old habits. And dreams don't happen if we live the same life that we always have.

As Winston Churchill once said, "To improve is to change; to be perfect is to change often." Reaching a dream requires change and to make that happen an action plan is critical.

For some of the first dreams lists I made, taking action immediately was not part of the process. I've found when a person immediately builds a plan to take the next steps on a dream, they achieve far more. So, I fixed my process. The second iteration had a system for action plans.

When Brookelynn and I do our dream planning at our dreams date every year, we have an action kit ready. It includes credit cards, calendars, and computers. This tactic is an important step, and skipping it is a big mistake. Taking immediate action isn't just a good idea, there's ample science to prove it.

Dr. Carol Dweck's research shows that when someone believes they can achieve a goal, they are more likely to do it successfully. Our beliefs bring about behaviors (and responses from others) that lead to the outcomes we desire. This is why nailing down what actions to take to accomplish a dream is a critical step.

Dweck's studies also found a correlation to a willingness to work hard for that achievement. Manifestation happens when an idea becomes more real. An action plan helps to facilitate this process.[22]

Most dreams never are realized simply because people don't take any action. The ones that do come true sometimes are realized through happenstance, luck, or a crisis. Think of a fifty-five-year-old man who planned to get in shape in his thirties, but never did.

The heart attack he has while waiting in a cruise buffet line might terrify him enough to change his french-fry habits into a lettuce-leaf and exercise lifestyle. Dreams often happen when people fall into them out of circumstances or desperate need for change. The idea behind this is to change your dreams from a someday phenomenon into your everyday life. That's where you will maximize your return on the dream-planning time you invest in.

There's also a bonus. Your quality of life gets an immediate boost. That pleasant dream buzz becomes persistent when you always have something to look forward to.

THE POWER OF DREAM PURSUIT

On our annual dream-planning date, Brookelynn and I start with a review. We pull out our phones and scroll through our photos from the previous year. It's a handy record of the dreams we've accomplished. And we use the review to write a list of the year's awesome highlights. We make a list of the things that we really enjoyed, the places we went, and even the people we spent time with. We then go through our Google Calendars to pull out other highlights that we'd like to repeat the next year.

We always complete the session by both agreeing that it was the best year of our lives. It feels cool to be able to say that because action planning has become an unequivocal part of the process. Sometimes we'll notice there are times where we didn't really have a plan. We took the girls and we did an awesome, epic hike that turned into an all-day outing. Now the impromptu day of awesome becomes a structure we schedule and repeat.

The pursuit of these dreams is really where the juice is. When I have these targets written on my list that I'm working toward, it brings so much purpose to those in-between stages.

If there's no action taken, I might be motivated for a day or two, but nothing's really going to change in the long-term.

How the Dream-Planning
Process Works

Once a group completes Stage 2—Dream Sharing & Stealing at your retreat, the next session should be Stage 3—Dream Planning. Remember to give participants some time to relax in between sessions.

Schedule a two-hour meal break with downtime and games before starting the planning session. If it is an overnight retreat, run the planning session the next morning. Let people have time to give their brains a rest. They'll need to reset before they launch into planning.

When everyone is back in their seats and refreshed, I start by getting them back into a good place. We review their lists and I acknowledge the great work that they've already done. I recognize and appreciate their "all in" attitude, the vulnerability that they operated with, and how they supported others.

I also ask if anyone has had a dream come to mind since the last session. During the break many people have conversations that spur the creation of new dreams.

When everyone is refreshed and ready to go, I introduce this next phase with this statement:

There has to be action in anything that we do to achieve a dream.

Planning is a pivotal part of the strategy, so I explain that we could sit around the table and dream up these great ideas of things that we want to do, but if we never take action then the list remains just a list. There must be a system to ensure follow-through.

First, reassure people that they are not taking action on all one hundred items on their list. Instead they are going to chunk it down, get practical. And the whole plan does not have to be completed there and then. You'll review three steps to take big dreams and distill them down into smaller, micro actions:

Step 1: Dive into the list.

Step 2: Research and break down the steps.

Step 3: Plan it and take action.

Step 1: Dive into the List

The first step is to have participants select the dreams where there is a possibility that they could make them happen within twelve months. Have them reduce their big list down to five, ten, fifteen, or for ambitious go-getters maybe as many as twenty. Encourage them to scan through all the categories and choose doable dreams and the ones that excite them most. Each person works independently to decide what dreams they are most excited about being able to accomplish.

Everyone has a different level of drive and ability. Each person's financial resources are also unique. Some of the dreams on their list will be things they can pull the trigger on that day and others will be larger commitments.

Step 2: Research and Break Down the Steps

It's beneficial to explain to the group that most things on their list are very attainable and often times within reach, we just need to figure out what steps to take. If they can metabolize this idea, then you've done a great job. The other concept you want them to understand is that anything is possible if you break it down into smaller steps.

For example, if someone has always wanted to learn to fly a helicopter, get them to ask "what would I need to do to fly?" It may seem simple, but helping them to ask the "How?" is really important.

Then they would need to break down the steps:

1. Find a flying school and learn the cost and dates of upcoming sessions.

2. Source the finances needed.

3. Sign up.

4. Start classes.

There are obvious advantages to gaining these action skills at work. Companies today need to innovate, to come up with big ideas. Many companies today are focused on using agile teams to achieve projects. The agile approach is a process where teams break down a large project into smaller tasks and take action on each task, adjusting and adapting as they go, until the project is complete. This strategy is very effective because a team concentrates on micro tasks easily to achieve a larger goal.

In a similar way, with dreams, the best way to figure out what to do next is to reverse engineer the master dream. You start from the big idea, and reflect on where you are now and where you want to go. Then, discern waypoints on the journey to completing the project.

So, taking action immediately can look a number of ways. It can simply be research or scheduling a time to research. Maybe it's booking a time to have a conversation with a key person who needs to be on board with a dream so it can happen. Some dreams are tied to finances so a person might need to do some financial planning or save funds or secure a loan. If they have the funds, then of course they could decide right then to book a flight, buy a membership, or pay for a course.

I worked with a colleague, Elliot, who, during a dream-planning session went online to TD Ameritrade and opened a Roth IRA. He invested $6,000 that day. He said he had always wanted to get into investing but never actually took the time to do it. He was pretty happy with himself after he had done it. The entire room was thrilled too. It was spectacular.

Another person on our team, Alex, wanted to take his father to a Minnesota Vikings game that year in Seattle. So for Alex, taking action meant making a phone call to his father during this session to see if the schedule would work and to propose the idea.

One last example: Two members of our team, Colleen and Hailey, both had Tulum on their list of places they'd like to visit. So they decided on the spot that they would go and vacation in Tulum together.

This is a great time for people to be researching races, trips, online courses, and many other things.

Step 3: Plan It Now

At this point, you'll start to see people pop out of their chairs as they realize how they've been stalling on taking basic actions. In one of my events, a woman said she had been talking with her husband about organizing a girls' weekend for her old friends from college. She said it had been a conversation for four years, but no one had done anything about it. So she decided to take it on, and engaged in the planning using her training from the retreat. She started by setting a date after gaining some consensus from her friends, and planned it from there. Small actions make dreams simple. Achieving a big dream happens from performing a collection of small, sequential actions.

So here is the list of immediate actions you can share in a dream-planning session:

- Research.

- Call a friend/family member to discuss one of the dreams.

- Block out time or schedule appointments or conversations on a calendar.

- Make purchases.

- Share with a partner or accountability buddy.

- Launch a group.

- Create a group for dreams action plan accountability.

By this point people start to get pretty excited. Everyone is booking things; they're doing it out loud. "Hey, I just booked concert tickets to see Taylor Swift!" Other people get excited for them. So they call to find out dates and rates to take a local art class. And so it goes.

Your role as a facilitator is to cheer them on and keep saying: "Okay, what else can you take action on now?" Sometimes a person will need support to make a big idea smaller. Walk around and ask questions. What are you looking at right now on your list? How can you chunk that down and make it smaller so you can take action today? What action can you take on that one right now? Anything else you can do today on that one?

The idea is to have people leave with at least two or more plans in their calendar scheduled for the next three or four months, so that their dreams are made more possible and easily achieved. This increases the odds they'll follow through.

CLOSING OUT THE RETREAT

In the event wrap-up, I ask people to share a dream that they're going to get done in the next three to six months. Anyone can opt out here, but in my experience, most step up. It is infectious. Again this goes back to the idea of sharing and accountability; when a person says, "I booked singing lessons," their colleagues are more likely to ask, "Hey Ramsey, how's the singing going? Karaoke on Thursday night??"

My hope is that you get hooked on this process and follow it yourself the rest of your life. If you leave the event and take action on selected dreams in the ensuing three or four months, you will accomplish a dream or two just like that. It is that simple. And it's like a good drug. Keep it up and five years later you're blown away by the life you're living.

I've seen this happen again and again. When I read through the feedback from my team, here are some highlights of what they said...

Colleen shared:

"My first Dreams Retreat completely altered my idea of what I can create for my life. I left feeling wildly energized to cross off my dreams and it gave purpose to my everyday actions."

Alex said this:

"Since my first Dreams Retreat I've purchased a house and completed a marathon. I now own a couple shares of Apple stock and can touch my toes. I've achieved many dreams by the age of twenty-one simply because I'm able to show up where I work and look at it not as a job, but as a vehicle to creating the life of my dreams."

Nik had this experience:

"The Dreams Retreat enabled my team and I to think BIG, BOLD, and truly live life by design."

BEYOND THE RETREAT: KEEPING DREAM ACTION TOP OF MIND

Once the Dreams Retreat ends, people will go back to their normal routine. But now they will have new actions to take that will excite them. To keep the dreams alive, and the motivation levels high, there are useful simple structures to put in place. In this section, we'll cover basic tricks to keep the momentum around dreams that were built in the workshop live day-to-day. This will also reinforce the dreams culture you are building.

Snap-on Cadence of
Dreams Communication

Any company that implements this dreams-planning system and runs a Dreams Retreat also has a responsibility to keep the concept of dreams alive.

Even if no further action is taken after the event, it is still worth the time together. Each team member will have created dreams lists and deeper bonds, and will be more compelled to take action. Obviously, better yet, and what any leader should want, is when a person continues pursuing dreams.

Dreams should be kept top of mind beyond the Dreams Retreat; otherwise the work that's been done might become wasted time. That's where you can use a strategy I call "snap-on moments of dreams communication."

The process is simple. Talk about dreams at every opportunity. Sprinkle in dream talk during meetings, in updates, and in other forms of communication conducted in everyday business, but keep it simple. Tack on five minutes for dream discussions to most large group meetings and some small ones. Again, you don't have to go crazy. Five minutes is all you need.

I usually talk dreams at the opening of a meeting during a vision-casting segment. For any meeting that I run, I start by grounding the group in who we are as a culture and what our mission is as a company, and get everyone to remind themselves how the conversation about results matters. During this time there are usually projections about where we're headed and what we're doing that's on brand for our company vision. I always take a moment to recognize a handful of people who have gotten some dreams done recently.

For example: "Hey guys, I want to acknowledge Cheryl today. Last week, she got adult Invisalign braces, which is on her dreams list. It was something she wanted to do for a decade and she's saved up and planned. We had a virtual meeting where she was smiling and showing it off."

It's really that simple. One day it's Cheryl. The next day it's Mike and his wife, who are building their dream home. Next week it's Brad, Jamie, and Dean. One is learning to play the guitar, while another just got back from Costa Rica, and the third became a mentor for Big Brother Big Sisters.

These little dream sprinklings are tremendously inspiring. They also inspire people to keep taking action because they have evidence that dreams do come true. Of course these group conversations encourage a continuous peer-to-peer dialogue, which is incredible to see form.

Embrace Continuous Dream Sharing and Structures

A company can take dreams to the next level by initiating structures such as community bulletin boards, WhatsApp Groups, or other online forums, although it's not totally necessary since those conversations tend to happen organically. If the leadership is inspired to do this to keep dream conversations alive, then do it. However, keeping it opt-in is not a bad idea either. And you might find some people have a looser approach to dreams. That's okay. Keep it fun to think about and pursue. Don't make it an onerous mandate. You want to drive it through inspiration not by edict. Also, avoid dream shaming. Too much pressure can cause people to feel stressed and not want to take action.

Refrain from a "get it done" mentality. Instead, recognize people for their dream accomplishments. Celebrate awesomeness in both team conversations and private ones between a manager and teammate.

Encourage managers to share their dreams and invite their teammates to share their lists if they feel comfortable. Once again, make it opt-in only. Don't force anyone to participate. There's value in people figuring out for themselves why they are sharing or not, or taking action or not.

If a person gets to the end of the year and there is all this talk of dreams at the company and their colleagues are high-fiving over their personal wins, those on the sidelines will no doubt have a revelation. Maybe they are scared. Maybe they struggle with commitment. Maybe they realize they don't really know what they want because they haven't focused on themselves for a long time. These types of realizations happen and they help a person recalibrate, learn, and get better at their performance in life and at work.

Patty McCord, former Chief Talent Officer at Netflix, wrote in her book *Powerful: Building a Culture of Freedom and Responsibility*, "Most people really appreciate the opportunity to get a better understanding of their behavior."[23]

Dreams have a way of revealing to a person what might be holding them back in other areas of life. If they didn't take action on a dream, it might be because they are indecisive, or struggle to be outcome driven. Or perhaps they realize they don't value themselves enough to make pursuing dreams a priority. All these personal reflections can surface in response to how a person accomplishes, or doesn't accomplish, their dreams. These are valuable insights that offer growth opportunities for a more fulfilling life.

Commit Company Resources

One persuasive thought to plant inside of any work team is that if they share, the company will help them achieve their dreams. For this the company must be willing to contribute resources, which will build a stronger affinity between employee and company and improve retention. When the company knows the dreams of its people, it can play a key role in making those dreams come true by awarding them with vacations or dinners or VIP tickets that perhaps an employee wouldn't otherwise do for themselves. We'll talk more about corporate incentives in detail in Chapter 7, but before we get there let me plant one seed about community conversations around dreams.

Themes emerge during a Dreams Retreat. Groups often form naturally during peer-to-peer interaction. The leadership team should be listening because the company can provide additional community support with announcements and sometimes resources.

For instance, let's say a good 40 percent of the room attending a Dreams Retreat reveal they have major health goals that year. If you see that happen, look for ideas on how you can support the common goal. Maybe you come across the announcement of a Tough Mudder event in your city—that's an endurance event series in which participants attempt ten- to twenty-mile obstacle courses.

It's fun. It's tough. And it's a great goal to put in front of your health and fitness dreams people. If the company is able, it might up the ante with an incentive where the company pays 50 percent of the sign-up costs to anyone who wants to go.

The leadership team can take small actions like this to support the team. Think about it: who doesn't want extremely health-conscious people working for them? These employees tend to have more energy, think clearly, set boundaries, and overcome overwhelm.

In the case of a Tough Mudder, to use my example, there are many physical and mental resilience skills a person needs to work on to take on that challenge. And doing it as a group is fun and easier than if someone did it solo. It also strengthens team bonds. There is intangible value for a company to apply corporate dollars toward dreams, and it doesn't have to be much.

SMALL WINS, BIG RESULTS

The bottom line on action is that small wins lead to big results. John Kotter, a well-known management consultant who is an expert on change management and wrote the book *Leading Change*, introduces an 8-Step Process for Leading Change within an organization. Kotter later updated the process in his

2014 book *Accelerate*.[24] One overarching theme of his extensive work is: "Wins are the molecules of results."

Kotter talks quite a bit about the power of small wins and using those wins to create examples for continued momentum on any team.

As a team starts accomplishing dreams, momentum builds for both the individual (the dream achiever) and the entire team. The individual experiences what it's like to set a target and achieve it. They then experience being recognized at work for living their life to the fullest. And every time the team sees this, they are reminded of their own lists. It brings the focus back to them. This perpetuates the dream achievement cycle.

Keeping dreams alive is critical for the success of this system and, as you see, it only requires small regular efforts. It's also a great way to know more about what everyone is up to.

Consider what it's like to work for a company that not only helps you dream but is willing to incentivize and throw corporate dollars at high-performing team members to make their dreams happen. I can tell you; it's amazing.

CHAPTER 7

CORPORATE CONTRIBUTIONS AND DREAM INCENTIVES

A GOOD FRIEND OF mine works for a billion-dollar company. She's not in a C-level suite, but she does really well there. For Christmas her company gave her credits to spend on items in a corporate catalog to recognize her for her hard work that year.

Now, you would think a billion-dollar company would reward its performers with things like a weekend for two at a luxury spa, an upbrand mountain bike, or gift cards to buy concert tickets, or even deluxe bedding. Something with a bit of a wow factor.

One day we sat there in front of her laptop, browsing through the branded items she could choose from. She was given a login to an online portal, which housed a preselected gallery of items to spend her credits on. What popped up was: A desk clock. A laptop bag. An insulated to-go mug with a super grip (available in go-go green, punk pink, or bright blue!) for the coffee she might bring on her commute. Of course, all the items were branded with the company logo.

She chose the desk clock. A compact "Made in China" desk clock, perhaps to count down the hours before she could bail from her job and work for a company that had a little more imagination.

Needless to say, when the clock was delivered, she showed it to me and we had quite a chuckle. But the laughter had an undertone of bitterness. It was a gesture that her company created this points process and online catalog. I say gesture, and not a nice gesture or an awesome gesture. Someone in the company had rubber stamped the project thinking it was a good HR practice. "The deluxe desk clock is the new addition to this year's Triple Diamond Incentive Catalogue. They're going to love it!"

It probably cost thousands of dollars to plan and set up too. Sadly, this kind of "perk" went far beyond what so many large companies bother to do. It's depressing. John Ruhlin talks about the negatives of most corporate gifts in his book *Giftology*. John shares many horror stories similar to this.

She was a great employee; her company had made an effort to acknowledge her but in a way that seemed corporately self-interested. Many businesses do this. The corporate catalog might have once seemed like a good idea to incentivize people to perform. Earn your credits! Get cool stuff! Let's be honest, most people love to rack up an insane number of points in loyalty programs. You earn 1,000 points for every $100 you spend. It seems great. Eventually you get to 500,000 points. Yay you!

But then you discover you qualify for one free night at an efficiency hotel chain. Free breakfast served in the lobby every day. De-luxe.

Some companies do it better. They allocate a decent budget for employee incentives that they can use for travel destinations, or substantial gift card incentives, even fancy cars in some cases. While it's nice, it's not uniquely shaped to what that person truly wants. Because you are a top performer, we are giving you a deluxe all-expenses-paid ski package in Aspen! Yeah, but I don't ski. Oops.

A company might also incentivize an employee with funds for education. For instance, it might pay for a person to get their MBA. That is an incredible move on the part of any business. They're hoping that investment will have a direct return.

A highly prized employee with serious credentials and skills will do more to move the company's bottom line. Don't get me wrong, it's obviously great for the employee too.

Now consider what it's like to receive any gift, at work or even in your personal life, that is an item you were desperate for and had put on a personal list. You've probably experienced this before, maybe at Christmas, so it's probably not a stretch. One year your big get is a smart self-flying drone, something you'd never buy for yourself out of the family coffers, but a cool tech toy you'd love to have. Or maybe you said to your partner, "Don't get me anything this year for my birthday. Let's just book a two-night stay at the Ritz Carlton downtown." And your spouse makes it happen. How awesome is that? You get exactly what you wanted. No effort on your part required besides sharing that you want it and being awesome in the relationship.

It's amazing to get a gift that is on your list rather than picking something from a catalog. Any company with a dream-planning process has a massive advantage. They can use corporate dollars to fulfill dreams that have a serious impact. It blows the corporate catalog level of ROI out of the water.

CORPORATE INCENTIVIZING WITH DREAMS

As a leader, I often feel that when a teammate shares their dreams list I get access to a cheat sheet that contains all the hot buttons for that individual. So for a company, it makes great sense to spend money on this. It takes the guesswork out of deciding where to spend company money when it comes to employee incentives. They get what they want and I can support them to help them achieve what they want. As a company leader, I build a deep affinity with the employee.

The Value of
Sincere Appreciation

The night John came to the corporate banquet I'd never seen him look so slick. His thousand-dollar J. Hilburn suit was all class.

The custom-tailored charcoal suit was matched with a white crisp shirt underneath and simple black tie. It was the first custom suit John had ever owned, and it was paid for by the company, a thank you for the work he'd done that year. He'd hit incredible sales milestones.

John had never been a serious shopper. Like most guys he kept it simple. He always dressed well, but never with a signature style of any kind. Usually he wore a black or grey shirt with jeans or khaki pants. Yet, when the company underwrote his first visit to a tailor for a custom-fitted suit, he experienced shopping as he'd never known it. A saleswoman had fawned all over him, color matching ties to his eyes and complexion. He loved the experience. He loved the suit. And I loved that he loved the suit. Gifting suits or dress shirts became a big trend of mine.

But again, I'd only give a suit if it made sense. Just like tailoring clothes to a person, I saw the value in tailoring dreams. When company dollars are invested in a person with something they want, they feel seen, heard, and appreciated. It builds a tighter rapport and the appreciation is reciprocated. The person works harder because they know the company will help them achieve more dreams, but they also feel valued.

To understand what a person wants, a manager has to engage with them at a level that goes deeper than performance goals and objectives on the annual review. When a manager asks what an employee wants long-term in life, the center of that conversation is the employee. These acts of listening, interest, and appreciation make a massive difference in the relationship between the manager—and by default the company—and the employee. They also correlate to higher levels of performance.

According to research conducted by Officevibe on the Global State of Employee Engagement, 96 percent of employees want to hear feedback regularly and only 43 percent of highly engaged employees get feedback weekly.[25]

Appreciation is what teams need and want. And dreams are a simple way to make it happen and make it more personal.

Retain Your Superstars

It's challenging to leave a company that makes your work and personal life better. Retention is another worthwhile benefit that comes from personalized dreams incentives. People want to be in relationships and environments with structures that make them feel good and further their growth. There's nothing that's not positive about a company helping their people achieve their dreams.

My colleague Matt explained our dreams culture this way: "When you're growing as a person, you want to keep the people helping you accomplish those dreams around you."

Matt isn't the only one. While most people spend a couple of years in a job and then jump ship for a new opportunity, people on my team struggle to leave. That's because our culture has made their lives so much better.

During the process of writing this book I sent a survey out to my team to collect information on the dreams they had achieved because our company had put dollars behind them.

Seth had been gifted so many fun experiences, from hanging from ceilings to jumping on trampolines, to escape rooms to breweries, to hotels that give out cookies. One year he and his wife received warm monogrammed bath robes; another time they spent a night out in Chicago for a shopping spree there.

K.C. wrote about receiving his dream to travel outside of the US. He traveled to Cancun and to Australia/New Zealand. K.C. also received a dream trip and told me this about it: "I was able to see the first ocean of my life."

Smaller dreams have been gifted too. Nik was given a Tempur-Pedic Cloud mattress. Not bad to have an employee get a great night's sleep.

They keep dreaming and achieving and playing bigger and bigger each year.

Then, what's incredible is they share their wins with friends. They share how their company helped them achieve their dreams too. They share on social media. Now suddenly the talent pool available to Cutco is growing. This is another way corporate-funded dreams are great for the brand image. The dream talent stays and naturally attracts new recruits using word of mouth.

Attract New Talent Through Word of Mouth

Word of mouth is the best way to find new talent. When my boss, Mike, was taken by a passage in *How Google Works* by Eric Schmidt and Jonathan Rosenberg,[26] he sent me a note that said: They believe in personal recruiting. In the book, Schmidt says Google always asks their employees, "Who do you know that is truly exceptional?"

We live in a social media-driven world where personal achievements are on display publicly. Guess what employees do when they have a dream fulfilled? Post it on social media. If you take your first flying lesson on the company dime, you bet you're going to post airplane pilot selfies. And if somebody asks in the social back and forth on that post, "I guess you like where you work!" then you can bet the answer is going to be an enthusiastic endorsement of the company culture that has far more impact than any recruiting ad.

Beyond Company ROI

Giving a gift that someone wants feels amazing. It's wonderful to be part of a moment in time that leaves a mark on someone forever. It's a life-changing experience for the giver, for the receiver, and for the company, to say we helped deliver that outcome.

When a person achieves a dream they can become a dreamer for others. They share their accomplishments and make others believe they can have their dreams fulfilled too. You may be wondering how that is done. Let's explore that next.

HOW TO OFFER DREAM INCENTIVES

Incentivizing with corporate dollars that fund employee dreams might seem like a simple process. Mostly it is. But the best way to use dreams as incentives is to stick to three guidelines:

1. Chunk dreams down.

2. Ask the dreamer.

3. Lean away from cash.

Chunk Dreams Down

I struggled in the beginning with dream incentives because some items on dream lists were huge. It wasn't in the corporate budget to buy Ted a $200,000 cabin cruiser. Or fund Jessica's trip to Bali. And I really wanted to help Kelly start a side business, but there were so many facets to what she needed there too. The bigger the dreams, the more challenging it is to determine how to contribute with a fixed allocation for each person.

Dreams come in all sizes. So contribute in whatever ways you can that fit your budget. Smaller dreams like a dinner out at a Michelin Three Star restaurant are easy. So are tickets to a football game. When it comes to helping build a side business, perhaps you can fund a website branding package or give them a sizable gift of Google or Facebook ad credits. Those are no-brainers.

Large dreams can be a little more complicated. Still, there are ways to get creative and break them down. Consider the allotted amount of dollars and then use them on a portion of the item. For instance, if a "cabin cruiser" is on Ted's list, maybe you can pay for his boating license. The company buys him that, or if the budget allows, add the rental of a cabin cruiser for a day or a weekend for the new captain and family or friends.

Again, little efforts go a long way.

If a person wants to travel to a pricey destination, pay for their hotel for one or two nights, or buy them a gift basket that features a book like *Exploring Rome* and an Italian phrasebook or a license for an Italian lesson they can use on their phone. Or maybe they'd prefer a business class upgrade on their air ticket. Think creatively and when in doubt ask the dreamer what they want.

Ask the Dreamer

Make everyone's life simple by being straightforward. Go to the person you'd like to spend money on. Tell them, "Hey, I've got a certain amount earmarked that I was planning on spending on you. Do you have any trips that are coming up? I'd love to pay for your hotel for two nights." Or, "I'd love to take care of the flight for you." Or be open ended about it. Say, "Hey, I wanted to show you some appreciation for X, what do you want most right now?"

Better yet, get a copy of their dreams list. "Hey Evan, would you mind sending me your dreams list? I'd love to reference it so I can give you more targeted gifts and rewards."

If you have a deep relationship with the person, you might have conversations months ahead about the dreams they are working to fulfill. This makes it easier for you to spend dream money on them when the time comes to recognize them for their performance. Surprises are fun. It's nice to look at the dreams list and come up with a fun idea, though sometimes it's better to simply ask. Especially if you have a fairly healthy budget, you will want to get them exactly what they want. Then you know how to proceed because you should also avoid cutting checks or giving cash only.

Lean Away from Cash

Cash or a Visa gift card can get spent on other items outside of dreams. Paying for a new snow shovel or a child's snow pants is practical, sure. But not very dreamy.

Having a dream come true lights a person up in a way practical purchases can't. And, spending money on a dream fulfills the program's purpose and reinforces the dream culture that's being created.

Some dreams are intimidating. It's helpful to give an experience, task, or item related to the dream because it helps a person truly commit and get serious about making it happen. Let's say Lyne has been talking about writing a book for a long time. She's been upfront that it's a massive undertaking and writing isn't her strength. She is scared and has no clue where to start, but she also has a little voice in her head that's getting pesky. It's saying, "Lyne, when are you gonna write that book?" If the company buys her a writing course, she has a place to start. It's one simple accountability structure. And she'll likely go to the class both because she wants to and also because she doesn't want her boss or colleagues to see that she chickened out.

Also, how many times has someone gifted you cash or a gift card and you use it for someone else or something that's not a gift? Left to their own devices, people will use money and gift cards out of necessity and not thought. No one ever dreams of buying a ten-pound bag of potatoes. At least no one I know, yet.

So instead of providing a voucher, go ahead and book it for them.

Corporate Trips
That Check off Dreams

Let me close this chapter with a bit of a tall fishing tale. Not an inflated story about a mythical fish that may or may not have been caught. This one is about a massive fish that we actually caught on a business trip.

Corporate trips are great for checking dreams off lists. They are also great for planning group activities that give colleagues the opportunity to bond outside of work, have a dream experience, and lock in memories together.

A few years back, we had a Cutco rewards trip in Cabo San Lucas, Mexico. It's a resort city on the southern tip of Mexico's Baja California peninsula, known for its beaches, nightlife, and marine activities such as diving, sailing, and game fishing.

There were roughly seventy people in our group. I knew that many of the people on my team had "deep sea fishing" on their dreams lists, so I booked an excursion.

Lukas, who was one of the guys in our group that day, had never been deep sea fishing and was the most excited. So I organized a day trip and a group of us set out on a boat rigged with eight heavy-gauge fishing lines off the sides and stern. Game fish are notorious fighters so you need some tough tackle to land them.

It was a sunny, warm day on the ocean. One of those lazy, languid days that naturally slows down even the most ambitious Type A salesperson. To further help nurture a sense of relaxation, I had a cooler on board stocked with plenty of frosty Mexican beer.

Lukas had never gone deep sea fishing, but was known as a real outdoorsman. And he grew up in the Brainerd, Minnesota, area. Brainerd is located southwest of the westernmost tip of Lake Superior. The landscape there is dotted with fish-laden lakes. It's a fisherman's paradise.

So Lukas knows his way around catching fish, although a fresh-water catch in Minnesota typically can't rival the game fish that lurk in the warm salt waters off Cabo. The Minnesota state record is a 57¼ inch muskie, basically a long pike, if you know your fish. Not small by any measure when you consider that a typical catch in local lakes is measured in inches not feet.

In Mexico, the fish are bigger. Much bigger.

Out on Mexican waters, Lukas was third to cast that day and the first to catch a fish. He hooked a massive bluefin tuna. Now you may only relate to tuna as fish in a can or a chunk of red flesh on sushi rice. On average, Pacific bluefin tuna weigh in at 130 pounds and can swim up to seventy-five miles per hour. They are wild aggressive predators with razor-sharp teeth.

Lukas' tuna was a monster and he was ecstatic to hook it. He battled hard to land the giant fish, which was almost as large as him. No kidding here. It was five or six feet long and like a barrel at the thickest point on its belly. Lukas vibrated with glee, euphoric from the adrenaline of landing his catch.

After landing the fish with the help of the deckhands, he jabbered like a kid at Christmas. Bemused, amazed, and simply delighted. He then probably drank four beers in quick succession in an effort to calm himself down. It was hilarious to see his reaction. We have great memories of the awesome day—that giant fish was one of four we pulled out of the sea that day.

As you can see, delivering dreams to your hardworking employees is immensely satisfying. And, the experiences certainly become amazing stories to recount later to the entire group.

By the way, I call this spotlighting, and there's a very specific way to use this technique in your dreams culture. We'll talk about that in the next chapter.

CHAPTER 8

DREAM SPOTLIGHTING

RUNNING A MARATHON IS hard, finishing it is harder. But, as I mentioned earlier in this book, usually the route is lined with people wildly cheering the runners on. Besides achieving the distance itself, seasoned runners will tell you the crowd is one of the best parts of the race experience.

That's what Alex Funk was anticipating when he had "run a marathon" on his dreams list for 2020. Obviously 2020 was pretty unexpected and his plan to run a marathon was pushed back from summer to early fall, then he pushed it back again and finally decided that he was going to run a marathon regardless of all the races being canceled in the US!

Alex took his race indoors and decided to run a solo marathon on a treadmill in his aunt's small gym. He was very disciplined in his training and it helped him get into shape and continue exercising during the final four months of 2020.

One week before the race, we were in a virtual Zoom meeting together. He knew I'd run a marathon and so he asked me for some advice on how to get through it.

"What you need to do is to prop up a computer, have a Zoom meeting going the entire day, and send out the code to as many people as possible so that they can stop by and cheer you on," I told him.

He didn't take my suggestion seriously, though, as it sounded a little weird. I knew what it was like running 26.2 and I knew that people there to support the race is what makes the difference for the runners. Alex wasn't going to have any spectators or fans and I thought that was an unmemorable way to run a marathon. I kept pushing the idea of the Zoom marathon. He finally agreed to do it.

Alex got the computer set up and I sent around the Zoom code to as many work groups as I could early in the day. I showed up for the start of the race to wish him good luck and cheer him on. Then he was off. Starting slow and steady, finding an even pace in the first miles of the race. I hopped on the Zoom three or four times throughout his race to cheer him on and there were always a few other people present. Word spread in his personal life as well, and there were all sorts of people joining. He was never alone; it was pretty exciting. I decided to throw a Hail Mary and sent a personal text to our CEO Bruce Goodman.

Alex obviously knew of Bruce, since he is the CEO, but the two of them didn't have a personal relationship. I figured it was a long shot, but knew it would mean a lot if Bruce had time to pop in and say a few words.

I told Bruce that Alex is super important to me. Now Bruce knows of our division's culture and how we're fanatical about dreams, so I knew there was a good chance he might pop in. Then again he is a busy man, so I understood that it may not have been possible.

Then, Bruce stopped by to have a chat and encourage Alex. Later, when Alex took a moment to drink some water three-quarters of the way into the run, he also grabbed his phone and texted our manager group chat. My phone beeped and this text message appeared: "Bruce Goodman cheered me on! I can't believe this. I can't quit now."

We all had a good laugh about that.

At the very end of his race there were over twenty people there to watch him finish! It was such a team effort. Everyone was inspired. Alex finished the race and was elated. For days he kept talking about how he met Bruce Goodman for the first time. He couldn't believe it.

He also sent me a personal text that read: "The dream manager!!! Thanks for your encouragement and advice. This day is an accomplishment I'll remember for the rest of my life. Very special day that made it ten times more memorable with the Zoom idea. You're the best. Another dream down to finish my year."

Wow. It was one heck of a silver lining that came from a disappointing COVID-19 cancellation.

WHAT IS SPOTLIGHTING?

S potlighting team members is a simple and effective way to build an inspiring dream culture. And it's not usually done with a marathon and Zoom. It's much simpler to do.

To keep the dream culture alive and encourage others to continue to dream, the idea is to intentionally showcase dreams fulfilled as much as possible for others in your team who have also been exposed to the dreams program. This encourages people to dream more. It also reinforces dream achievements for the dreamer being profiled, and inspires everyone to continue to think big, which is also one key component of a thriving, high-performance work culture.

Without dream spotlighting the dreams culture can stall out. It's silly to say, but true; it's really easy for people to forget about the whole concept of living the life of their dreams.

Also, remember the dream system should be set up as an opt-in program and not made mandatory. Leadership should use it to expose people to the dreams idea and create an environment that encourages actions as a way to achieve a goal. Dream spotlighting accomplishes this.

Think of yourself as a gardener tending plants to encourage their growth. You're creating an environment, supporting it, and nurturing it. It's like watering your plants, or providing plant food or enriched soil where needed. If there are problems, you correct them. If someone is faltering, spotlighting provides support, like a plant stake. Provide the right growth environment and you'll find the growth happens organically.

The simplest way to spotlight is to take a commonsense approach that you would use when implementing any new program or system to a team. Make it part of what is already being done and piggyback it off your normal business routines and conversations.

Again, this is part of the snap-on communication strategy you learned earlier. As a general rule, match the formality of the event to the spotlighting you want to add. For instance, if it's a weekly meeting, you're going to share for five minutes about a few wins.

If it's an annual corporate dinner, maybe you spend fifteen minutes recognizing people for dreams with awards using a PowerPoint presentation or bringing them up on stage live. Daily you can use messaging in WhatsApp, Slack, or group text messages.

If a team member accomplishes something exceptionally cool, and it's fitting, you might want to have them speak for a moment. Just ask them to share a couple highlights. It's so simple, but it takes a bit of rigor and intention to turn it into a routine. But you'll want to do it, because there are substantial benefits for the company.

The Benefits of Spotlighting for a Company

Performance and celebration are closely linked,[27] especially in high-performance environments like in business and sports teams. In 2010, psychologists Michael Kraus, Cassy Huang, and Dacher Keltner conducted research on trust and cooperation, which are two key metrics of a high-performing team. The study concluded that the accumulation of celebration rituals boosted team performance. The more a team celebrates each other, the better they perform.

Spotlighting dreams encourages a culture of celebration. When people know what each person is out to achieve, and what they have achieved successfully, a dialogue opens. People get to know each other better, which leads to a more cohesive team.

A workplace that has a dream culture often becomes a safe place for people to talk openly about their pursuits without judgment. And I've found what happens is the opposite of judgment: unwavering support and the formation of deep bonds.

It's exciting to see somebody on your team win. When it's at work it's inspiring and we just want the best for the person. It's not like a competition, which can happen between colleagues if one is succeeding and the other isn't. It can happen in families, too, with siblings. When people are too close sometimes there's more judgment and competition because their success is seen as a threat.

Everyone loves a good hero story, so when colleagues share the achievement of their incredible feats, everyone feels inspired. There's an immediate buy-in when Paul from marketing shares his desperate dream to find a solution for his chronic fatigue. Then after seeing a sleep specialist he gets diagnosed with sleep apnea, is treated for it, and solves the problem, and feels like a new man.

By sharing at work, a support and accountability network often emerges among peers that helps the person succeed at meeting challenging goals. It's a winning formula.

Spotlighting helps develop deeper relationships among people beyond supporting their dreams. When a team does this around personal dreams, not only are they checking off more goals in their personal life, they become a force to be reckoned with at work.

A mentor of mine once taught me, "If you dislike someone, there is a good chance that you just don't know them well enough." It is easy to write someone off if you lack knowledge about their history and their personal challenges. As you peel back the layers and get to know somebody, you start to appreciate what makes them who they are. Then empathy comes naturally.

If Dale knows that Sharon is having a tough time in her marriage and she's dropped the ball on an email that needed to get sent to the community of clients, then he might step up and help her out. If everyone is accountable to each other and lends a hand when it's needed, our teams succeed, and their company succeeds too.

In times of disruption and innovation, successful, cohesive teams that have each other's backs have never been more important. Many companies survived during the COVID-19 crisis on the strength of their people and their ability to deliver results together in the face of difficult circumstances. These teams can only happen when people are deeply connected.

Dream spotlighting is a way to nudge that into existence, especially long after the day of the retreat where people share for the first time. And for the dreamer in the spotlight, it's affirming to be celebrated for achieving something that means so much personally.

The Benefits of Spotlighting for the Dream Achiever

When a person is spotlighted it validates the effort that they're putting in to develop their dreams. It reinforces and validates why the dream process is so valuable. When a person is acknowledged, they usually ride the high and take more actions on dreams. They will want to be spotlighted again and encourage others to have the same for themselves.

It's critical to be recognized for accomplishments. The validation builds confidence in people and helps them become bolder when they tackle a problem. It also always leads to better performance. It's wonderful to be recognized for their value outside of work too.

Consequences shape human behavior, and positive consequences, such as praise and reward, enhance performance.[28] Positive reinforcement is a long-standing principle of psychology and management, because the majority of employees want to be appreciated and recognized for their work. Spotlighting is one simple way to make appreciation happen.

HOW TO
SPOTLIGHT DREAMS ACHIEVED

T he process of spotlighting is fairly straightforward, but it holds nuances you should pay attention to. To dream spotlight effectively you must have:

1. A mechanism for sharing dreams achieved

2. A mechanism in place to find out when people accomplish their dreams

There are a variety of ways to dream spotlight. Companies should decide and use systems that best support their team dynamic.

A Mechanism for Sharing
Dreams Achieved

There's no stock mechanism for executing on a dream spotlight strategy. My best advice is just start doing it where it makes sense. Snap it on. Make it simple. Spotlight everywhere. Do it online, offline, with bulletin boards. Do it at meetings and large corporate events.

And always request a communication loop. Managers need to know dreams are being accomplished; otherwise they won't know to spotlight or incentivize with corporate dollars and dreams.

Be sure to add a little reminder at the end of a spotlight with, "Let your direct report know if there's a new dream on your list that you are focused on. And share it with your peers, because public accountability will help you achieve it."

There are many ways to encourage people to share their dreams. For example, entice people to share their dreams by mentioning an opportunity to use the next scheduled bonus toward fulfilling it.

Introduce people with similar dreams to link them up for personal accountability.

Encouraging people to share their dreams with others also keeps you in the loop when they happen, because word spreads. Exciting or inspiring dream projects can go viral. Look what happened with Alex Funk's treadmill marathon. If you spotlight them immediately after you discover a new piece of dream news, it will help the person stay in their bubble of inspiration even longer.

Show Don't Tell

There's a difference between showing and telling. Showing brings us into a moment, makes it real for us, moves us emotionally. Telling keeps concepts, well, conceptual.

Here's the difference:

Telling: I went for a thirty-minute walk on the beach at sunrise in Thailand. It was spectacular.

Showing: The first morning after I arrived in Thailand, I got up at 5:30 a.m. because I was jet lagged so I walked out onto the sugary white beach on the edge of the Andaman Sea. There was a slight smell of orchids in the air. As the sun rose, the red and orange light danced off the wavelets on the blue water. And in the distance, up on the sea wall I saw young monks in orange robes taking it all in. The experience was transcendent.

Ask the person to share. Or share and show photos or videos. Sometimes what may seem insignificant to someone may have a huge impact on someone else. Who doesn't want to go to Thailand after hearing a share like the one above? As mentioned before, if somebody accomplishes something really cool and it's fitting, encourage them to speak for a moment when you spotlight them, and provide a couple of highlights.

Share Your Personal Dream Wins

One dream on my list is to be the best dad I can. For me, that means teaching my girls about generosity, giving, and charity when you're in a position of strength. So in 2020, my wife and I sat down with our daughters and together we picked a charity that inspired them for the upcoming year. It was Youth Link, one of the only shelters in the Twin Cities that provides overnight sheltering for homeless children. I told ten managers about this charity at our first fall meeting in 2020.

Our girls raised money that year for sleeping bags and coats for the kids. With the support of my wife, we created a campaign to donate one hundred winter jackets. To teach our kids these values, we told them about the charity, then they made a video asking for money. They wrote a letter to potential donors. We also took them shopping to buy all the gear. Then we all went together to deliver it. With the support of many friends, family, and coworkers we raised about $1,500.

This dream meant a lot to me—and to my daughters.

As I often do, I opened a meeting by telling this story. It's the simplest way to spotlight and lead by example. A leader who is a proponent of a dreams culture needs to be taking action on their own dreams, so that they always have a handy example from their own life to share.

Don't make it always about your own dream wins, of course. Mix it up. But lead by example, and ensure you spotlight your own wins on occasion.

Staying Looped In on Dream Wins

We've already discussed systems for implementing a continuous dialogue on dreams achieved. We've talked about encouraging and engaging in your own dreams sharing as key to the strategy. But perhaps the simplest way to know when someone accomplishes a dream is to keep an eye on social media feeds.

Most colleagues are connected on Facebook and Instagram and have the ability to see the nonwork sides of their peers. If you have a younger crowd at your company, you might need to check different platforms like TikTok, so ask if you are unsure.

People will often post pictures of dreams achieved. This is where you'll find pictures of marathon finishes, travel photos, and event-related dreams sharing. Or that your colleague is a crafter with a new Etsy shop. Travel, speaking engagements booked, concerts attended...both fun and accomplishments get posted to social media. Usually there is a dream flavor to it all.

When you see a win on a social media feed it's a great conversation starter. Do some basic recognizance. Find out if this is a dream that the team should know about. Then get pictures, videos, and testimonials too so when you spotlight it it's vivid.

Depending on the relationship you can spotlight without permission.

There is one caveat, though. Sometimes you have a deep conversation with a colleague and know about a dream that might be private. If the dream is a touchy subject or if the person is usually quiet about their wins, ask if you can share.

If it's a weight loss goal, for instance, they might not want that advertised. Or a budding romance. A spiritual or religious goal might make them uncomfortable about a spotlight too. So keep the lines of communication open, and when in doubt approach the person you want to spotlight to get their permission.

Spotlight to Maintain
a Thriving Dreams Culture

Dream culture takes nurturing. Small actions. Little reminders woven into the day-to-day routine. These are the keys to success. Eventually you'll find there are so many dreams being achieved that it's tough to know everything and choose what to spotlight. When you experience this, you know you're doing something right.

Eventually you'll find, with a few simple actions taken regularly, the dream culture builds on itself. People start loving dreams just as much as you do and they can't wait until Dreams Retreat time every year. They then become leaders inspiring the next generation of leaders in your organization. It truly is remarkable how dreams spread like wildfire.

It's easy to be concerned about whether all this dream talk is too much. Does it take away from work? No. Remember how our revenue increased after we started working in a dreams culture. Is it too repetitive? Not by a longshot—it reinforces the culture. After the first large-scale Dreams Retreat back in 2017 this was a concern of mine. What I've found, though, is that people run with it. They look forward to the dreams, talk, celebrations, and doing the retreat again.

Those who are doing the process for the second time around are usually the champions. They spotlight themselves and other people. They are proponents that light the new hires up.

Keepin' the Dreaming Alive

After our first major Dreams Retreat I wondered if people would see value in repeating it the next year. Attendees already had created a dreams list at the first event, so I wondered if my rinse-and-repeat structure would be a bore. I've found that's not the case. It's actually the opposite.

First, not everybody plays full out the first time. While they've made a dreams list before, they have the advantage of having been with it for a year. Second-time attendees have metabolized the idea of dreams, so they are more open to it; they operate fully with 100 percent buy-in.

The spotlighting throughout the year, which may have included them, provides evidence that the program works because they have been a witness to many of the dreams that have been achieved. During the second time around, some people will level up on their dreams. Those who were shy, or the skeptics, the first year have a chance to open up and engage more fully. They have become more comfortable with the idea and they see an opportunity for themselves to achieve one or more of their unfulfilled dreams in the coming year. So they go for it, determined not to let it get away from them this time.

For the second timers, the Dreams Retreat is an opportunity to re-engage with their list, feel okay with not having done everything, and iterate on what they do want, this time with a greater commitment and willingness to take their dreams on.

I've also seen people who've crushed their first-year dreams list. They come back on a dream high because it is an opportunity to focus on and relive the dreams they achieved the previous year. They create new dreams, then take the planning part seriously. They know what's at stake.

From a leader's perspective, the second-time attendees are great to have back. You have some phenomenal stories to work with and spotlight. You want to begin the Dreams Retreat using examples from the year prior and showcase the second timers in the room who had big wins. Quite often the second timers take it up themselves to lead. They'll stand up and spotlight themselves.

There will, of course, be dreams that went unfulfilled. Be sure to avoid dream shaming here. In your spotlight process don't praise John, who delivered on his dreams, and then shame Danny, who didn't. Always frame it without morality. It's not good or bad. It just is what it is. Acknowledge that a person who achieved one dream is a winner. A person who delivered on no dreams is also a winner, because now there is an opportunity to identify barriers holding them back, and in more places than work. Maybe it's commitment that held them back. Or, making decisions about what they want. Or perhaps the place to put renewed focus is on allocating time to devote to their dreams. It's a growth opportunity and a chance to discover something new about themselves and transform it into a new behavior.

With an attitude of curiosity, they learn to deal proactively with failure. By accepting they didn't achieve some dreams, they can then evaluate why and recalibrate and try again. Certainly these are brilliant skills to have in business today. Innovating on products and services requires a willingness to fail and try again. Teams that embrace constructive criticism also grow better and work more effectively together. Often you'll find if they can overcome what is in the way in a dreams process, that issue will also be in play elsewhere in their life. It may be evident in their work habits, in their romantic relationships, or in their personal life. Someone who doesn't welcome new ideas and is cynical might also see that trait is also at play at work or in their marriage, dating life, or friendships. Not always, of course. But sometimes if they can catch themselves and bring a new behavior, it is a wonder to behold.

Any person who accomplishes even one more dream than the prior year will experience a substantial difference in who they are and how they relate to themselves. There's movement there. Acknowledge that. Remember, it isn't about going from zero to hero. This is about having the best year of your life in the coming year.

The retreat can be used as annual reflection time. That is something that most people have never had. If that is what they get out of it, it is so worth it.

CHAPTER 9

THE UNEXPECTED BENEFITS OF DREAM PLANNING

"DANE, THIS IS AWESOME," my colleague Ramsey said, with a grin that hadn't left his face all day. We were just getting off the flight that landed at JFK in New York City.

The day before, we were supposed to fly home from a conference at headquarters in Olean, New York City, with the rest of our crew. Instead, I'd rerouted us. I'd booked Ramsey and myself a flight to New York City for an extra night.

Ramsey and I had worked together for four years at this point. He was my Pilot Sales Manager that year, which is a one-year position at our company that's an apprenticeship role with management. He had been doing a great job and I wanted to show him my appreciation.

It's not uncommon for me to have access to many of my team members' Dreams Lists, so when I was looking to share my appreciation with Ramsey I went straight to his list. I knew I could give him a bonus, or give him a gift card, but that wasn't in line with our culture. Instead, I decided to surprise him and take him to see the Minnesota Vikings play the New York Jets at MetLife Stadium. What made this dream even more exciting for Ramsey is that it accomplished two dreams:

- Visit New York City and see Reuben, his brother

- Watch a Minnesota Vikings game in person

We were sharing a meal the week prior to the trip when I told Ramsey of the plan. "I've got a surprise for you," I said. "Next Sunday, instead of flying back to Minneapolis I booked us two flights to NYC. I'm taking you to a Vikings game. I got an extra ticket so you can invite your brother too."

"Are you serious? Like for real? This isn't a joke?"

Now, Ramsey is a guy who, in his early twenties, was a DJ for bar mitzvahs. He's a very passionate, charismatic character, and never holds back from saying what's on his mind. It's probably why being alongside him on this dream trip was so enjoyable and fun. Most days, Ramsey consumes life like a kid eating birthday cake.

So this day was amazing for both of us. Ramsey had an amazing day of reconnecting with his brother, catching the train to the stadium, tailgating, rooting for his team as they beat the Jets, and then being able to explore the city the next day.

As the gift/dream giver it was just as great for me. Watching Ramsey have an amazing day and knowing what it meant to him was a pretty great feeling. On top of that, I had the opportunity to catch a show at the *Comedy Cellar* in Manhattan, which is one of the best comedy clubs in the US. It had been on my dreams list for quite some time.

This was a special day that neither of us will forget.

The simple dream-planning framework came from my personal life. I brought it into my workplace in 2012. And I've since watched thousands of my teammates like Ramsey (and many of whom are my very good friends) achieve dreams that were once only inspired ideas that they had no real plans to make happen.

I have found more than once, when a dream is written down or shared with a colleague, a friend, or a stranger even, the rate at which a person achieves that dream speeds up. It's like magic. It feels as if the powers of the Universe are positively conspiring in the dreamer's favor. Once the dream is out there, synchronicities seem to occur.

While leading a dreams workshop for another company, a participant shared with the group that she wanted to take a burlesque class. Another participant chimed in and said she had a connection to someone that taught lessons and would connect them. Just like that, the dream was one phone call away from reality.

Every year I have moments like this. To date, I've checked off approximately fifty dreams since I got serious about dream planning in 2013. As a leader, it's been incredible to be along to experience the dreams of others, like Ramsey's dream day, Lukas and his massive tuna, and the custom bespoke suit for John.

Seeing dreams come true all the time, whether they are personal or of someone I care about, has expanded my quality of life. Certainly, it's only reinforced the dream concept.

When I launched my dreams process, you'll recall, my intention was to build a culture of empowerment. My focus was not entirely about benefits to the company's bottom line. I hypothesized that this natural byproduct of a high-performance team would be created by a dreams culture. But over the years, I've been astounded by the magnitude of unexpected benefits experienced by the company, myself as the instigator of the process, and the work community it has impacted. Companies with a dream planning system experience an astounding ROI that goes beyond revenue targets, though those are certainly included.

Lasting brand affinity is built, which raises retention and often draws in new top talent. When high performers grow out of their roles and move on to other companies, they never forget how the dreams culture shaped them. They speak highly of the company to peers in other businesses and people in their social sphere. Sometimes they remain lasting business partners and work with the company in new B2B capacities. As I was finishing up this book, I received a text from an old coworker who went through the dreams retreat with his wife. He sent me a link to a very nice RV and said "Look at what your dreams coursework did for us. $40k investment for my family's future memories!"

Beyond benefits to the corporate bottom line are the lifelong friendships that emerge as a result of our dreams culture. People want to stay connected to friends who encourage them to grow and succeed in life. It's astonishing to see how the dream life-style expands organically. The dream machine keeps humming.

In this chapter, I'll share about unexpected benefits. I'll do my best to convey how dreams truly transform companies and so many lives.

LASTING BRAND AFFINITY, HIGHER RETENTION, NEW STARS

Remember Connor and Kelsey, the couple who got married in Ireland? Connor worked with my division for six years and moved on to another company in 2019. While he was a part of our dreams culture, he and his wife ran with the concept.

I recently asked him about all they've accomplished. Connor had an original list of one hundred plus dreams that he's realized and he is still creating more each year.

"The company I work for now is great. They have a good culture and they really care for their people," he said. "With that being said, there's no tie into the bigger picture in life and what really gives work meaning. I think so many organizations fear that if they talk about a greater world outside of work, they'll lose you. That's the opposite of a dreams culture. I loved working with the North Star division because I knew that all my work supported my bigger picture and my managers were there to support me to achieve it."

Connor said he'll never forget his time working for our company. Though he's left, he speaks highly about the Cutco brand with his new colleagues, and in his social sphere, with family and friends. Connor and his wife continue to dream and check items off their list.

It's never bad to have former employees speak highly about the company after they leave. New business collaboration can come out of employees moving on, but staying in close contact. More than that, when a company has changed their life to the extent of fifty dreams, they'll be more inclined to look for ways to continue a working relationship.

When friends or family see Connor's constant parade of dreams on their social media they might also strike up conversations with him that link back to Cutco. Naturally, my division has attracted new star talent through word-of-mouth conversations.

Sarah is one teammate who is still with us but said she's always sharing about our work culture with everyone she knows. "It is now an obsession that I want to share with my friends and family. I love working toward my dreams," she said. Again, the affinity she has to the company she works with has others take note, even reach out to see if they can get a job with us.

Ramsey has also moved on. He worked for our company for six years. During that time he knocked twenty dreams off his list. I recently asked Ramsey how our dreams culture made a difference for him. He said even after leaving, the company thanked him for his hard work by giving him one last item on his list. "The company offered to pay for five singing lessons, even after I decided to leave the company," he said. Ramsey and I are great friends and still keep in touch quite a bit. He still checks off dreams and continues to inspire his new colleagues, friends, and family to do the same. I can't wait to hear that former bar mitzvah DJ sing. Maybe that will be a new dream profession for him one day.

Team members are constantly sharing about our dreams culture. We've seen increased retention and often get better talent through referrals coming through the door as a byproduct.

Dream Bonds to Team Bonds to Forever Friendships

People are more likely to build long-term friendships when they get to know a person on a deeper level. In Chapter 5 you learned how dreams strengthen bonds and why that's important. More than that, friends at work have a team dynamic where people are more mentally resilient.

During COVID-19, I didn't lose a single team leader. I run two different streams of the business—one where we recruit, one with teams that sell Cutco products at live events such as county fairs, home expos, builder shows, and others. During the pandemic, on the recruiting side, we'd never been busier. Both division operations and demands to join our team were off the charts. But the live-events arm of the business was suffering. And still we didn't lose one teammate.

What I know of dream culture is it helped people get through the toughest year we've ever seen.

When work slowed down team members were able to look at the pandemic as an opportunity to pursue more items on their dreams list. They were truly living the work-to-live, not live-to-work principle. When someone has a focus on dreams, their life isn't defined by their job. There is power in this.

The connection my colleagues had with their teammates also made everyone more resilient. We had each other. We leaned on each other for support. And, we all stayed too. No one quit. And perhaps even better, we didn't need to let anyone go.

It's fascinating to look at the research around friendships at work. One research study conducted by Globoforce shows that almost two-thirds (62 percent) of employees with one to five work friends said they wouldn't accept a new job offer.[29] For employees with six to twenty-five friends, that number jumps to 70 percent. So the bonds that have naturally formed have led to greater retention rates.

But it also strengthened the commitment to our division's over-arching mission during tough times. People banded together. Each teammate had personal and professional dreams they could anchor into, to remind themselves of their purpose when times get tough. One person with big dreams who has purpose is a fierce team member to have on a team. They raise the others up during times of weakness, reminding them of their dreams.

On one of my regular check-in calls, Robert Wicks, who runs an events-based business within our team, said he was having a bad year. But despite the drop in revenue his outlook was very positive because he turned his focus to dreams. "I've gotten more dreams off my list than I ever would have imagined because I was given more time," said Robert. He accomplished a dream of playing over fifty rounds of golf in a summer and achieving his best score ever, sub eighty.

So many workers struggled during COVID-19 because their environment put them in a crisis state. Immediately, workers had new issues they needed solutions for and fast, and it related to their financial survival.

Performance expert and bestselling author Steven Kotler wrote an article for Ted.com in 2021 titled "Three Science-Based Strategies to Increase Your Creativity," where he wrote: "Pressure forces the brain to focus on the details, activating the left hemisphere and blocking out that bigger picture. Worse, when pressed, we're often stressed. We're unhappy about the hurry, which sours our mood and further tightens our focus. Being time-strapped, then, can be kryptonite for creativity."[30]

After my call with Robert, I wondered what it would be like if every person had this same line of thinking during tough times. If every person woke up with a clear vision or guiding purpose that was pulling them, no matter what happens, they would approach life with a more optimistic outlook and keep going, because dreams are a way of life.

WHEN LIVIN' THE DREAM BECOMES A WAY OF LIFE

T hink of a dream you've achieved. Big or small. It might be the day you won first place in the spelling bee in the third grade.

It might be when you saved up enough money to fly your mom and dad to Mexico for a trip. Or the day you bought your first home. Now when you sit in it and admire it some days, you might reflect on when it was once a dream. There are no words to describe how great it feels to achieve a dream. The closest word, maybe, is: miracle. Living any dream is joyful, wonderful, and magical. And it can be more than a once-and-a-while phenomenon. It can be a way of life. I've watched that happen to hundreds of people.

Up until I wrote this book, I didn't fully grasp the magnitude of how a simple dream-planning system that I deployed back in 2013 positively transformed so many lives. In the process of writing this book, I sent out a survey to my team to collect their answers for how our dreams culture has made a difference for them. They deeply moved me and re-emphasized the importance of this book and process.

One question I asked was: What dreams have you accomplished as a result of our division's dream culture? Give me all of them, even the small and weird ones!

Matt accomplished this:

Buy a house. Move to the Twin Cities. Run a half-marathon. Go skydiving. Vikings game forty yard line, Row eight. Solo trip to Amsterdam and Lisbon. Make it down the hill without falling on a snowboard. Visit an all-inclusive resort and swim with dolphins. Pass the fundamentals of Engineering exam 5+ years after graduating college. Be a BIG for Big Brothers Big Sisters. See a bunch of concerts I've always wanted to (Maroon 5, Dierks Bentley, etc). Zipline in Central America. I'm on my way to obtaining a black headband for Tough Mudder (to do this you must complete ten full courses and I've done six). And smaller personal goals like: Reading one book per month every year. A schedule for calling certain family members frequently to build better relationships. Help at least one other person accomplish a goal every year.

Working out (I can do over one hundred pull-ups in an hour-long workout these days), and continually trying to move up and get promoted at work.

Rachael's done this:

With the flexibility of work I have been able to travel to the Apostle Islands. I grew my communications skills to more effectively talk with friends and family and be more transparent. Save money and also invest money for retirement. I have a Roth IRA (I struggle with this when I have easy access to funds so having a savings account that I can't have direct access to was a dream). Paid off my car loan four months early. Became a better fur baby mom by shifting my schedule so I stay home more and spend more time enjoying my dogs. Run my own business before the age of thirty.

Here are Bobby's dreams achieved:

Bought a BMW. Traveled to Rome, Venice, Switzerland, Iceland, London, Paris, and many more dream places. Dogs. We have two Pomskies, which is my wife's dream dog breed. (They are amazing.) Home. We are building our dream home with custom built everything designed by us, including: French doors, ten-foot ceilings, luxury finishes, over 4,000 sq. ft., rear walk-out, mature trees, an acre of land, heated floors, island in the closet, a walk-in pantry, full Breville spread (espresso, coffee, and tea maker), massive 5 × 8 and 5.5 × 10 windows, a sauna, a custom made "river run" kitchen/dining table, pool table, 75" TV with Dolby surround sound, a wine nook, wet bar, reading settee, and more! Learned how to successfully "fell" trees with a chainsaw. Learned to count cards. Made money with stocks. My wife has her dream job and got her dream vehicle (a Tahoe).

These are only three responses of hundreds of people living dream lives. It's truly spectacular. And really it got me thinking, what are the all-time rough calculations on dreams achieved in the North Star division since we started? I did the math.

It's 2021 now, and I launched this process in 2013. From 2013–2016, you'll recall, I did it with the management team only. This was a group of approximately eight to ten people. At the high range, most people achieve roughly five to eight dreams a year. At the low end it's one. So the average, let's say, is four. Here's the calculation:

(4 Dreams × 8 Managers) × (3 years) = 96 dreams

A rough calculation shows that the managers in the initial years achieved a total of ninety dreams. Then, from 2016–2021, you'll recall, the dream process grew and we brought it to the entire division with the annual Dreams Retreat. While our vision grows and shrinks, on average we're about fifty to one hundred people that participate fully in the Dreams Process. Let's use fifty to stay conservative. So, that equation looks like this:

(4 Dreams × 50 People) × (5 years) = 1,000 dreams

Now, add all years together. Since this process began, 1,096 dreams have likely been achieved. And I'd say I'm being conservative here. I'm not factoring in the partners or spouses, or the dreams I personally achieved prior to the launch of the dream-planning process in 2013. I'm also not factoring in the fact that for every person who achieves one dream the rate at which they achieve dreams grows. It might even double because when a person achieves one dream they get excited, see value in the process, and keep going. Sometimes one dream achieved also helps them get to the next faster because they use the same process for producing results. So again, for each person, dream achievement is more of an exponential progression than a linear one.

Okay, and what if every dream achieved inspires one person outside of our division to check a dream off their list. That would mean that the actual amount of dreams achieved is 2,192. And this is not taking into account the team members who eventually leave our team but take dream planning with them.

A college student by the name of Jacob worked for Cutco in my division, where he was introduced to the Dreams Culture. He spent a few years with us and then went on to another career in the insurance industry. He built a very strong, high-producing team at Farm Bureau Services using the exact same dream-planning method. He helped his people create their lists and it became a focal point of their team.

Although it might be tough to quantify dreams achieved, I'd say these calculations are pretty accurate. They also show the tremendous impact dreams have on people's lives. If you ever thought dreams were fluffy ideas, now there's no way anyone can dispute their value.

DREAMS MAKE LIFE AND WORK WAY FUN

All cultures are created, some intentionally and some not. Once upon a time in 2013 I had a dream to build a culture of empowerment. More specifically, what that looked like to me is the experience best captured in this quote by American author James A. Michener. He wrote:

> The master in the art of living makes little distinction between his work and his play, his labor and his leisure, his mind and his body, his information and his recreation, his love and his religion. He hardly knows which is which. He simply pursues his vision of excellence at whatever he does, leaving others to decide whether he is working or playing. To him he's always doing both.

Since launching the dreams concept my work has become way more fun. It's play. And the team dynamic I experience is a judgment-free community where each person authentically wants the best for their colleagues. It's truly remarkable.

While writing this book, I wanted to see if my teammates felt the same, so I asked them another question about our culture: Describe any observations that you have about differences of working within our dreams culture compared to working at another organization.

Alex answered:

Working inside of dreams culture allows me to have purpose behind every single action I take. I understand why I'm doing what I'm doing. So I have tunnel vision.

Last, because I'm constantly making my dreams come true (literally!) I always know that there is light at the end of every tunnel. This allows me to PUSH and GRIND constantly and enjoy the rewards of my hard work.

Kelsey wrote:

With the dreams culture, work and personal life are tangled into one. There is a lot more depth to conversations as well because people are focused on achieving dreams outside work walls. It creates relationships with peers and the team. At both large corporations and smaller startups there is usually a lot more focus on work vs. home and a very basic level of "how was your weekend?"

Ramsey said:

> People outside of our team don't work on themselves to the
> same capacity. Sure, many people are growth-oriented, but
> very rarely do I come across people who have an active and
> working dreams list.

Dream planning isn't simply a fun hobby. Dreams make life worth living. They are a person's access to a life of constant fulfillment. There's nothing better than living a life where you can look back, see the results you have produced, and acknowledge, "This year was better than last."

Workplaces, and the world at large, need people who think big and chase their wild, inspired ideas. But for this to happen it starts with one person who shares and spreads dream living with others. I wonder now, could it start with you?

Leaders must do their own dream planning before they launch a dreams-planning process or workshop, or ever lead a Dreams Retreat. For the process to work, I can't stress enough how important it is for the program leader to lead by example.

You can't be an advocate of a program that demands people go after their dreams if you don't start with you. Leaders must do the work. It's important. For you, and for them.

REFERENCES

CHAPTER 1

[1] Matthew Kelly, The Dream Manager: Achieve Results Beyond Your Dreams by Helping Your Employees Fulfill Theirs (New York City: Hyperion, 2007).

[2] Michelle Gelfand, "The Secret Life of Social Norms," filmed October 28, 2018, in Palo Alto, California, TED Video, 17:45, https://www.ted.com/talks/michele_gelfand_phd_the_secret_life_of_social_norms.

[3] Saul Mcleod, "Maslow's Hierarchy of Needs," Simply Psychology, last modified December 29, 2020, https://www.simplypsychology.org/maslow.html#gsc.tab=0.

[4] "Kurt Lewin," British Library, accessed May 13, 2021, https://www.bl.uk/people/kurt-lewin#.

[5] "Lewin's Leadership Theory Explained," Leadership & Performance Partners, June 1, 2019, https://leadershipandperformance.com.au/leadership-development/lewins-leadership-theory-explained/.

CHAPTER 2

[6] "Understanding the Teen Brain," University of Rochester Medical Center, accessed April 23, 2021, https://www.urmc.rochester.edu/encyclopedia/content.aspx?ContentTypeID=1&ContentID=3051.

[7] Naveen Jain, Moonshots: Creating a World of Abundance (Moonshots Press, 2018).

[8] W.B. Kirchner, "TPN vs. DMN—Neural Mechanisms and Mindfulness," Exploring The Business Brain Model, July 6, 2017, https://exploringthebusiness brain.com/tpn-vs-dmn-neural-mechanisms-mindfulness/.

[9] Roger E. Beaty, et al., "Creativity and the Default Network: A Functional Connectivity Analysis of the Creative Brain at Rest," Neuropsychologia 64 (November 2014): 92–98, DOI: 10.1016/j.neuropsychologia.2014.09.019.

CHAPTER 4

[10] Stephen Bradley, "The Framing Effect: Influence Your Audience By Setting The Context," Vanseo Design, June 7, 2010, https://vanseodesign.com/web-design /framing-expectation-exposure-effect/.

[11] Nai-Wen Chi, Yen-Yi Chung, Wei-Chi Tsai, "How Do Happy Leaders Enhance Team Success? The Mediating Roles of Transformational Leadership, Group Affective Tone, and Team Process," Journal of Applied Social Phycology, 2011, 41, 6: 1421-1454, https://citeseerx.ist.psu.edu/viewdoc/download?doi=10.1.1 .452.2717&rep=rep1&type=pdf.

[12] Katelyn N.G. Young, et al., "The Role of Hope in Subsequent Health and Well-Being for Older Adults: An Outcome-Wide Longitudinal Approach," Global Epidemiology 2 (November 2010), https://doi.org/10.1016/j.gloepi.2020.100018.

[13] Martin Reeves and Jack Fuller, "We Need Imagination Now More Than Ever," Harvard Business Review, April 10, 2020, https://hbr.org/2020/04/we -need-imagination-now-more-than-ever.

[14] Seth Godin, Linchpin: Are You Indispensable? (New York City: Portfolio, 2011).

[15] Timothy T.C. So, "The Three Degrees of Influence and Happiness," Positive Psychology News, November 18, 2009, https://positivepsychologynews.com /news/timothy-so/200911185246.

CHAPTER 5

[16] "Life Lessons: Finding Happiness," YoursWisely, January 15, 2021, YouTube video, 1:17, https://www.youtube.com/watch?v=Kj8f2102mm8&t=7s.

[17] Jim Collins, Beyond Entrepreneurship 2.0 (New York City: Penguin Publishing Group, December 2020).

[18] Keith Ferrazzi and Noel Weyrich, Leading Without Authority (Redfern, New South Whales: Currency, May 2020).

[19] APA Dictionary of Psychology, "Impression Management," American Psychological Association, accessed April 23, 2020, https://dictionary.apa.org/impression-management.

[20] Kathy Gurchiek, "Survey: Workplace Friends Important Retention Factor," SHRM.org, December 16, 2014, https://www.shrm.org/resourcesandtools/hr-topics/employee-relations/pages/workplace-friendships.aspx.

CHAPTER 6

[21] Marshall Goldsmith and Mark Reiter, Triggers: Creating Behavior That Lasts—Becoming the Person You Want to Be (Redfern, New South Whales: Currency, May 2015).

[22] Tchiki Davis, "What Is Manifestation? Science-Based Ways to Manifest," Psychology Today, September 15, 2020, https://www.psychologytoday.com/us/blog/click-here-happiness/202009/what-is-manifestation-science-based-ways-manifest.

[23] Patty McCord, Powerful: Building a Culture of Freedom and Responsibility (Silicon Guild, January 2018).

[24] John Kotter, Accelerate: Building Strategic Agility for a Faster-Moving World (Boston: Harvard Business Review Press, April 2014).

CHAPTER 7

[25] "Mind-blowing Statistics on Performance Reviews and Employee Engagement," Clear Company, September 10. 2019, https://blog.clearcompany.com/mind-blowing-statistics-performance-reviews-employee-engagement.

[26] Eric Schmidt and Jonathan Rosenberg. How Google Works (New York City: Grand Central Publishing, September 2014).

CHAPTER 8

27 Christopher Peterson, "Team Celebration and Performance," Psychology Today, December 23, 2010, https://www.psychologytoday.com/us/blog/the-good -life/201012/team-celebration-and-performance.

28 Bob Nelson, "You Get What You Reward: A Research-Based Approach to Employee Recognition," American Psychological Association, 2016, https://doi .org/10/1037/14731-008.

CHAPTER 9

29 Kathy Gurchiek, "Survey: Workplace Friends," SHRM.org, December 16, 2014, https://www.shrm.org/resourcesandtools/hr-topics/employee-relations/ pages/workplace-friendships.aspx.

30 Steven Kotler, "3 Science-Based Strategies to Increase Your Productivity," Ideas. TED.com, January 28, 2021, https://ideas.ted.com/3-science-based-strategies -to-increase-your-creativity/.

CPSIA information can be obtained
at www.ICGtesting.com
Printed in the USA
BVHW030313061121
620880BV00003B/19